HAZAARON
KHWAHISHEIN AISI

Samineh x

HAZAARON KHWAHISHEIN AISI

THE WONDERFUL WORLD OF URDU GHAZALS

Selected, Edited and Translated by

ANISUR RAHMAN

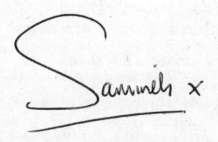

HarperCollins *Publishers* India

First published in India by
HarperCollins *Publishers* in 2019

Building No 10, Tower A, 4th Floor, DLF Cyber, City Phase II,
Gurugram 122002
www.harpercollins.co.in

2 4 6 8 10 9 7 5 3 1

P-ISBN: 978-93-5302-339-3
E-ISBN: 978-93-5302-340-9

Typeset in 11.5/16 Scala at
Manipal Digital Systems, Manipal

Printed and bound at
Replika Press Pvt. Ltd.

Hazaaron khwahishein aisi ke har khwahish pe dam nikle
Bahut nikle mere armaan lekin phir bhi kam nikle

ASADULLAH KHAN GHALIB

Desires in thousands I had, for each I would die
With many I had luck, for many I would sigh

Translation: ANISUR RAHMAN

CONTENTS

CONTENTS

FOREWORD

TABISH KHAIR

Originating probably as love poetry in Arabi[1] and transmuting vigorously across Asia, Africa, Mediterranean Europe and parts of eastern Europe over more than a millennium,[2] the 'ghazal' has been used in Urdu not just to pen love verse but also many kinds of religious, metaphysical, philosophical, realist and political poetry. Anisur Rahman's introduction, notes and careful sample of Urdu ghazals from across five centuries illustrate the background, richness and malleability of this genre so well that I have no need to cover that ground. But the true extent of Rahman's achievement in this anthology cannot be understood without reference to some matters which are often not discussed even by connoisseurs of the ghazal form—and more so in English where, both as translation and

---

1 Suggested by the etymology of the word.

2 See Rahman's preface for comprehensive details.

as borrowed genre, the ghazal has been growing in strength in recent decades.[3]

Part of the problem is the nature of the two languages—Urdu and English. For instance, like many other languages, Urdu is not policed by punctuation as much as English. Traditionally, punctuation marks were conspicuous by their absence in Urdu and even today, borrowed from the inevitable Latin regime, they appear rather sparsely. Hence, Urdu remains a language of inflexion and nuance, not rigid punctuation.

Any bid to translate Urdu ghazals into English that does not take into account this crucial difference is bound to be limited—and, unfortunately, even some excellent translation efforts of the past have tried to 'correctly' punctuate the English versions in ways that are bound to reduce the flexibility of their Urdu originals. One way to understand this is to remember that in the absence of punctuation marks, the meanings of a phrase of the ghazal, especially the repeated rhyme/refrain, can be nuanced. For instance, take this 'sher' by Ghalib (who is usually very good at playing with intonations and nuances):

Na tha kuchh to khuda tha kuchh na hota to khuda hota
Duboya mujhko hone ne na hota main to kya hota

---

3 Here, the role of the late Indian and Kashmiri poet Agha Shahid Ali and books like *Ghazals of Ghalib*, edited by Aijaz Ahmad, which contained ghazal-inspired 'transcreations' by W.S. Merwin, Adrienne Rich, Mark Strand and others, has to be stressed. In his preface, Rahman also lists a number of major anglophone poets who have adopted or adapted the ghazal form.

Translated into punctuated English, this would read more or less like this:

*When there was nothing, there was God; had there been nothing,
there would've been God.
I was destroyed (sunk) by coming into being; had I not been,
what would have been?*

Unfortunately, even if we forget the negation (*na*) this sher builds on and starts with, and similar matters, the punctuation of the lines in English reduce the nuances of the sher. In the original, Ghalib is not just saying (in the second line) that we are destroyed because we come into being, or lamenting the fact of his personal unimportance in a world of such magnitude. These are the meanings that are easily excavated in punctuated English. But in unpunctuated Urdu, Ghalib is making other and, to my mind, deeper points, which is also in keeping with his philosophy: he is suggesting that *nothing* could have existed if he had not come into being. This he does in at least two ways again. One of them is the tongue-in-cheek poetic persona of grandiosity that he often assumes, as does, for that matter, Shakespeare in his sonnets. The other one is the greater metaphysical point that for us, as conscious beings, the universe exists only because we exist. In that sense, 'what (*kya*) could have existed if I had not come into being?'

The tyranny of punctuation cannot be totally resisted in an English translation, but Rahman makes an interesting and admirable attempt to reduce it. He needs to be praised for taking the risk.

Then, of course, there are simpler matters, such as the
tendency of many translators to turn the ghazal's 'sher' into a
rhyming (or unrhymed) couplet. This comes naturally to literary
writers of English, a language whose alleys, if not roads, are
cobbled with couplets, but it does a cardinal disservice to the
ghazal form: the sher is not a collection of couplets that rhyme
aa, bb, cc, and so on. Instead, structurally, it is a poem with
one rhyme/refrain repeated: aa, ba, ca, da..., and at its best this
repetition both involves the audience and challenges/surprises
it. Rahman has paid attention to such matters and managed to
suggest the beauty and power of the original ghazals despite
the pressures of contextualized translation.

Not just in English but also in neighboring and overlapping
linguistic-cultural traditions, such as those of Hindi and Bangla,
Urdu ghazals and their writers have often enjoyed popularity
at the price of being reduced to loving caricature. The common
image of the Urdu poet—almost always a writer of ghazals—
can be described with three 'L' words: lover, loser, lamenter.
Anita Desai's major novel, *In Custody*, provides a version of this
stereotype in English. Actually, it often seems that if you write in
English about Urdu poets, you cannot escape this stereotype—
and one can find it in Bangla, Hindi and probably other Indian
fiction too, accessed from Orientalist sources.

There is an element of truth in this stereotype: Urdu
poets, especially writers of the ghazal, have sometimes tried
to cultivate the Triple L persona. But the element of truth is
only valid to the extent that it would be valid to see English
Romantic poets as unpractical nature-lovers lolling around in
meadows sniffing roses and daffodils! The ghazal tradition is
myriad and varied: the Triple L cult leaves most of it obscure.

It implicitly or explicitly leaves out the philosophical, political, realist, 'sacrilegious' and plainly irascible bits! Even authors like Asadullah Khan Ghalib, who cultivated the Triple L persona at times, also went beyond it: at his best, Ghalib's ghazals are philosophical and political in ways which are sometimes difficult for scholars to acknowledge even today. Some of Ghalib's shers would get his head chopped off in certain vocal circles today, and he was writing well before the early twentieth century, when the rise of poets like Mohammad Iqbal and Faiz Ahmad Faiz infused obviously political and radical commentary into the ghazal tradition.

It is a feature of this anthology that it conveys the malleability (in form and content) of the Urdu ghazal to the reader. That alone makes it a distinctive contribution and one of the reasons why it should be read by anyone interested in poetry.

The ghazal form has seeped out of Urdu and now exists independently in probably all major languages of north, west, east and central India, with its latest addition being snooty English. The reasons for this are various, but one of them is definitely the fact that Urdu ghazals have embraced the Indian subcontinent right from the start and continue to do so. This is worth remembering, especially today.

'We have broken a mosque and made a temple,' Mahesh Patel, a Hindutva supporter, told a news reporter in the summer of 2002. He added, 'We used hammers. Muslims should not live in India. They should go to Pakistan.' But the building that was torn down by Hindutva fanatics on 1 March 2002, one of many demolished during the infamous anti-Muslim riots in Gujarat, had not been a mosque. It was the tomb of a seventeenth-century poet, sometimes called the

Chaucer of Urdu poetry.[4] Vali Mohammed Vali, also known as Vali Gujarati and Vali Deccani, had died in Ahmedabad in 1707 and the tomb had been built for him by the residents of the city. It must have been a tribute to his popular poetry as well as recognition of his love for the region of Gujarat, which he had praised in his ghazals.

Deccani is one of the poets included here. His grave might have been destroyed, but his poetry lives on—as does the ghazal form in which he wrote about his places and times. Rahman's anthology enables the reader to dip into and sample this rich world of letters, imagination, emotion and thought. To the best of my knowledge, it is the first anthology that offers a comprehensive introduction to the entire history of Urdu ghazals in English, something made possible by the high level of Rahman's scholarship and his felicity in both Urdu and English.

---

4 If purists complain and point out that Urdu came into being only in the eighteenth century, they ought to be made to read Vali Deccani: his language can be more easily understood by ordinary speakers of Urdu today than Chaucer's English can be understood by contemporary speakers of English! (See Rahman's note under 'Metaphysical Beginnings' too.)

PREFACE[1]

Ghazal: Pretext, Text, Context

Pretext

'Ghazal' is an Arabic word which literally means 'talking to the lady love'. It is also a literary form, a quintessential mode of poetic expression that has passed through a unique trajectory in and beyond the Orient. For more than a millennium and a half now, it has been defining and redefining itself through times as distant as the classical and the modern, and climes as dissimilar as the East and the West.

---

[1] Some parts of this preface are drawn from my essay 'On Translating a Form: The Possible/Impossible Ghazal in English', *Translation: Poetics and Practice*, New Delhi: Creative Books, 2002.

1

The mid-sixth century which saw the emergence of the
mu'allaqaat, or the golden odes[2] in northern Arabia, witnessed
the beginnings of what subsequently came to be known as
the ghazal. Written in veneration of the pre-Islamic Bedouin
tribes and as paeans to their patrons, these odes, or *qasidas*,
also narrated the romantic hankering of lovers in separation,
and thereby became the staple material for the development of
the ghazal in the subsequent phases of Arabic literary history.
Interestingly, the ghazal did not emerge as an independent form
of poetry but only as a part of a larger tradition of the golden
odes. It had its origin in *nasib*, the erotic prelude to those odes,
and was meant to be recited to an audience. True to the spirit
and aesthetics of poetry designed for a community of listeners,
this prelude was strategically placed at the beginning of the odes
and was composed in light and musical metres. To arouse the
interest of the listeners, it narrated the experiences of romantic,
erotic and homoerotic love and longing for the beloved left
behind. It gave the poet an audience already allured and ready
now to be treated with a fare of odes on a variety of themes
concerning the Bedouin life and culture.

---

2 The golden odes, or *mu'allaqaat*, are supposed to be the earliest
   specimens of Arabic poetry. They acquired such popularity that
   they were inscribed in letters of gold on pieces of linen to be
   suspended (as the word *mu'allaq* suggests) on the walls of the
   Kaaba in Mecca as masterpieces of poetic art. Seven such odes by
   Imru al-Qais, Tarafah, Zuhayr, Labid, Antara, Amr ibn Kulthum
   and al-Harith are supposed to have been grouped together by
   Hammad ar-Rawiyah, who collected the early Arab poetry in the
   eighth century.

In the ages that followed, the ghazal acquired greater ground, both literally and metaphorically. It developed independently and found a suitable clime for itself in Persian, Turkish and other Oriental languages, before it moved out of the Orient and traversed in various directions to become a major part of larger literary traditions of different lands and languages.

The trajectory of the ghazal is unlike the trajectory of any other literary form that has had a history of traversing beyond its spatial confines. A brief tour through the passages of this poetic form and its diverse routes would reveal both the uniqueness and the universal appeal of this form. When the ghazal moved out of the Arabian Peninsula, it found a hospitable space in medieval Spain where it was written both in the Arabic and the Hebrew languages. In yet another instance, we have the ghazal reaching out to west African languages like Hausa and Fulfulde. Even while these ghazals developed their own marks, they also kept close to the Arabic model by retaining the traditional Arabic metres and forms. It was only when the ghazal reached Persia in the middle of the eighth century that it started developing its own contours even while it did not entirely disengage from the formal patterns of the Arabic ghazals. Later, the Persian ghazal acquired its definite character when it developed its own stylistic marks in refurbishing the *matla*, the first sher of the ghazal, and evolving a pattern of refrains (*radeef*) as the last unit of expression in the second line of each sher. It also defined the length of the ghazal from seven to fifteen shers, and made way for the poets to use their signature in *maqta*, the last sher of the composition.

Abdullah Jafar Rudaki, the first canonical ghazal writer of Persia towards the end of the ninth century, was followed in chronological order by other major poets like Sanai Ghaznavi and Fariduddin Attar in the twelfth century, Sadi Shirazi and Jalaluddin Rumi in the thirteenth and Hafiz Shirazi in the fourteenth century. The Persian ghazal matured further after the classical models in the subsequent centuries but it always distinguished itself for two of its most distinctive qualities: its acute mystical preoccupations and its keen philosophical concerns. The ghazal written in Persian, the dominant literary language of central Asia and India, made remarkable impact and proved quite consequential in the development of the ghazal as an archetypal form of poetic expression in the East. Even the poets who wrote in other languages looked towards Persia for mature models. Turkey, for example, being another destination of the ghazal, offered yet another variation on the Persian ghazal. Ali Shir Navai of Afghan descent, who was supposed to be the founder of Uzbek literature, brought it closer to new linguistic habits and exposed it to the extinct Chagatai language of Turkey in the mid-fifteenth century, and Fuzuli brought the ghazal to Azerbaijani Turkish in tone and tenor at the beginning of the sixteenth century.

Outside Arabia where it originated, and Persia where it matured, it was in India that the ghazal found its most hospitable destination. Even though the ghazal in India is sometimes traced back to the thirteenth century in the works of Amir Khusrau, its Urdu incarnation is rightly identified in Mohammad Quli Qutub Shah towards the latter half of the sixteenth century, and Vali Deccani in the succeeding century. Looking back, one may clearly notice that it has passed through several stages of development in form, content and language, ever since its first flowering in the Deccan and its subsequent branching out in various directions of India. While prominent literary centres like the Deccan, Delhi and Lucknow created competitive conditions for the development of the ghazal, several others spread over the length and breadth of the country championed their own features of style. All of them contributed together in constructing a larger and comprehensive tradition of ghazal writing which has kept growing ever since.

The most remarkable feature of the ghazal in India which stands out quite prominently is that the poets of various linguistic, regional and religious affiliations joined hands to broaden its thematic and stylistic frontiers and impart it a unique resilience that has stayed with it through all the phases of literary history.

The ghazal, as a literary form which has no other approximate form in any of the literatures, has long elicited the attention of poets writing in several Western languages. When the Orient lured Germany in the nineteenth century, the ghazal reached there with the translations of Persian works. Friedrich Schlegal, an Orientalist who studied Sanskrit, chose to make his bold experiments in this form. His contemporary, Johann Wolfgang von Goethe, imitated Persian models, translated ghazals, and wrote under the Oriental influence and published his collection, *West-ostliche Divan*. We also have, in the same line of descent, Friedrich Rückert, another Orientalist, writing his ghazals and publishing them in *Ghaselen*. August Graf von Platen, a master of twelve languages, is yet another example who practised this form, adhered to the Persian form of rhythm and rhyme through his *qaafia* and *radeef,* and published his collections *Ghaselen* and *Neue Ghaselen*. In modern times, the Spanish poet Frederico Garcia Lorca wrote his ghazals, called *gecelos*, and included them in his last collection of poems, *Divan del Tamarit*, which also reflected his ever-abiding interest in Arab Andalusian culture. The appeal of the ghazal travelled in other directions as well, which is exemplified by compositions in languages as diverse as French, Italian and English.[3]

In modern times, the ghazal found its larger acceptance in the English-speaking world. Adrienne Rich, John Hollander and Robert Bly in America, Jim Harrison, John Thompson, Phyllis Webb and Douglas Barbour in Canada, and Judith Wright in Australia are just a few of the many poets who brought the ghazal to new literary spaces, as they experimented with this form and made way for many others to emulate. On being introduced to Ghalib during the death centenary year of the poet in 1969, and on translating his ghazals,[4] Adrienne Rich developed an instant liking for the form. Later, she wrote her ghazals independently and published seventeen of them in *Leaflets* as 'Homage to Ghalib' and, subsequently, nine more in *The Will to Change* as 'The Blue Ghazals'. In her *Collected Early Poems*, she acknowledged her debt and wrote: 'My ghazals are personal and

3 Ghazals are also said to have been composed, for curiosity's sake, in several other languages like Bosnian, Esperanto, Norwegian, Pashto, Polish, Rumanian, Russian, Swedish and Ukranian.

4 Adrienne Rich, along with W.S. Merwin, Wlliam Stafford, David Ray, Thomas Fitzsimmons, Mark Strand and William Hunt, was introduced to ghazal and its major practitioner, Mirza Asadullah Khan Ghalib, by Aijaz Ahmad who gave them the literal translations of some of Ghalib's ghazals, along with explanatory notes. They, in turn, composed their own 'versions' of the poet. See *Ghazals of Ghalib*, New York: Columbia University Press, 1971.

public, American and Twentieth Century; but they owe much to the presence of Ghalib in my mind: a poet, self-educated and profoundly learned who owned no property and borrowed his books, writing in an age of political and cultural break-up.'[5] Similarly, the ghazal caught the imagination of John Hollander to the extent that he defined its poetics and wrote a ghazal on the ghazal, a kind of definitional piece, following the strict discipline of the form with its *qaafia* and *radeef* falling in place.

At a remove from Rich and Hollander, we have quite a few Canadian poets making their forays into this form. Jim Harrison, who published sixty-five of his ghazals in *Outlyer and Ghazals*, was aware of the Arabic and Persian ghazal tradition and knew of Rich's excursion into this form. He is one of the more prominent poets to discover the ghazal and find space for all that he considered crude and queer to write about, along with all that was normal and natural. 'After several years spent with longer forms,' he said, 'I've tried to regain some of the spontaneity of the dance, the song unencumbered by any philosophical apparatus, faithful only to its own music.'[6] Another poet, John Thompson, in his carefully crafted ghazals in *Still Jack* also valued the freedom that the ghazal afforded, but he did not mistake it for surrealist or free association poems violating a sense of order. Instead, he valued them as 'poems of

---

5 Adrienne Rich, *Collected Early Poems: 1950-1970*, New York: W.W. Norton & Co., 1993, p. 426. (*Leaflets* and *The Will to Change*, published in 1969 and 1971 respectively, are included in *Collected Early Poems*).

6 'Notes on the Ghazals', Jim Harrison, *Outlyer and Ghazals*, New York: Simon Schuster, 1969, p. 26.

careful construction performing controlled progression'[7] with no deliberate design upon the reader. He found in it a way to test the limits of imagination that might lose the track of reason, if left unguarded. Yet another variation in the writing of the ghazal may be seen in Phyllis Webb's *Sunday Water* and *Water and Light*. She evolved the concept of 'anti ghazal' and found in them a space for 'the particular, the local, the dialectical and private'.[8] She degendered the form and resorted to a subversive way by de-valorizing the female figure, which the ghazal had been traditionally valorizing ever since its inception. A much more radical position was adopted by Douglas Barbour in his ghazals included in *Visible Visions* and *Breathtakes*. He chose to try the limits of sound and form by modulating breath as a mode of expression and bringing it closer to performance poetry. With this entirely new mode of apprehension, Barbour added yet another facet to the fast emerging body of the North American ghazal. 'Indeed, a very particular sound, for example, caught my imagination,' he said, 'when I thought of ghazals, the sound of breathing itself. There was a form and there was a breath. And there appeared what I call the breath ghazals.'[9] Compositions by Douglas Lochhead in *Tiger in the Skull* and Max Plater in *Rain on the Mountains* may be read alongside the compositions by the North American poets.

---

7 *Still Jack*, Toronto: Anansi Press, 1978, p. 5.

8 'Preface', *Sunday Water: Thirteen Anti Ghazals*, Victoria: Morris Printing Company Limited, 1982.

9 Anisur Rahman, 'In a Thick and Rich Soil for Writers: An Interview with Douglas Barbour', *Odyssey*, Vol. V and VI, 2004, p. 6.

The prominent Australian poet, Judith Wright, who began as a traditionalist, turned quite experimental towards the end of her career when she too experimented with this form in a section, 'Shadow of Fire', containing ghazals in her collection, *Phantom Dwelling*. In her departure from the traditional ghazal, she maintained thematic continuity in her couplets and gave her compositions a title. Like all other poets, she too executed a variety of experiences in her couplets like the experiences of warfare, birth, growth, decay, contemporary life and the inevitability of the human fate. In the hands of all the poets mentioned above, as also many others who practised this form, it may be marked that they treated the ghazal with great respect and curiosity. It was an immigrant form for them in which they saw the prospects of simulation and assimilation to enrich their own poetic capital. They saw in it the possibility of exploring newer areas of experience that could be expressed in manners hitherto unknown in the European tradition.

Carrying the argument further, I should like to assert that the ghazal in English acquired its definite face and form with Agha Shahid Ali who wrote his own ghazals, but more importantly, he created a condition for the poets to write their ghazals, observing its formal requirements. He despaired over the way poets treated this form as a way of writing free verse, which he thought was a contradiction in terms if one wanted to write a real ghazal. Considering their efforts 'amusing',[10] he brought them face to face with the rigorous demands that the ghazal

---

10 Agha Shahid Ali, (ed.), *Ravishing Disunities: Real Ghazals in English*, Hanover: University Press of New England, Wesleyan University Press, p, 1.

made. Compositions by Daine Ackerman, John Hollander, W.S. Merwin, William Matthews, Paul Muldoon, Maxine Kumin, Keki N. Daruwalla, to name just a few, included in his *Ravishing Disunities: Real Ghazals in English*, amply show how far the ghazal had moved towards meeting the rigorous demands of the form after Ali's intervention.

Considering the above examples, it may be asserted that the ghazal in English has been approached and appropriated variously. Thus, it could not be the same as it is in the Arabic, Persian and Urdu languages. It could only be a different ghazal. At best, it could be a declaration of a different creative stance, a different poetics and a different way of broadening the frontiers of literary exchanges. It donned many a garb as it travelled in many directions, was played by many hands and grew in many ways. In the process, it was identified as 'tercet ghazal' by Robert Bly, 'bastard ghazal' by John Thompson, 'blue ghazal' by Adrienne Rich, 'breath ghazal' by Douglas Barbour and 'anti-ghazal' by Phyllis Webb.

Text

Currently spelt as 'ghazal', this poetic form of Arabic origin has been variously written in various locations as 'ghazel', 'ghasel', 'gazal', 'gazalo', 'gasel', 'gacelo' and 'ghuzzle'. Even though its formal features have remained the same, there have been variations in the style of its composition, as it has gone beyond the spatial confines of Arabia and Persia in particular, and the East in general. Before considering its nature as a literary form, let us consider its essential features. The ghazal is a collection of at least four independent shers, it is written in a single metrical frame and it uses the same rhyme scheme preceding a refrain throughout the composition. The first sher, called *matla*, has a given scheme of rhyme and refrain in both the lines but the subsequent shers do not have the rhyming phrase in the first line. An example of two shers from Ghalib should make the point:

> *Dil-e naadaan tujhe huaa kyaa hai*
> *Aakhir is dard ki dawaa kyaa hai*

> *Hum ko un se wafaa ki hai ummeed*
> *Jo naheen jaante wafaa kyaa hai*

The rhyming words, *huaa, dawaa, wafaa* are called *qaafia* and the recurrent phrase, *kyaa hai, kyaa hai, kyaa hai* is called *radeef*. The last sher, called *maqta*, often bears the signature of the poet in any of the two lines, where he either addresses himself or speaks to others through a persona to impart the ghazal a sense of completion. The architectonics of each sher is interesting. Even though both the lines are thematically interconnected, the first line brings about a sense of pause with the last phrase and it makes way for the following line, even without an enjambment or a break of thought. As the first line extends into another and brings about a sense of completion, sometimes it also springs a surprise on the reader and holds him in pleasant awe. Composed as thematically independent shers, the ghazal does not have the unity of a regular poem, yet it shows an organic development and internal unity of its own. There are, however, instances where the shers are thematically interrelated and one sher leads to another to complete an idea. Since the given metrical design does not allow an extra syllable,

the poet is put to severe test in order to express himself within
the available space of a sher. As such, the beauty of the sher,
as also of the entire ghazal, lies in precision and in the art of
achieving that precision. To achieve this quality, the poet can
only work through understatement and concrete images, mixed
metaphors and implicated symbols. Further, the remarkable
worth of the ghazal lies in creating a condition of music and
configuring a visual structure with all the shers having the same
line length. As such, a ghazal is a musical unit on the one hand,
and a hieroglyphic representation on the other. It knows no
beginning, no middle and no end. It is a literary representation
that has not turned archaic in spite of its long history. It has
matured with cross-breeding between cultures and languages,
and forms and genres. It is a non-finishing project, an ever-
moving kaleidoscope of poetic composition which has grown
with the passage of time, sher after sher, ghazal after ghazal.

Ever since its origins in Arabia, the ghazal has been
assiduously engaging with the ideas and ideals of love in all
their romantic and divine manifestations. It has been a site
of socio-political concerns and metaphysical-cum-mystical
engagements, even as it has afforded open space to the
mundane and the ordinary. During its development in the
Arabic-Persian tradition, it has acquired its own features of
reference and has institutionalized the traditional concepts of
union and separation, ecclesia and monastery, the censor and
the guard of faith, the beloved and the idol, the lover and the
rival, the messenger and the confidante, the tavern and the cup
bearer, and so on. Apart from enjoying a place of pride in the
literary domain, the ghazal has also thrived in social spaces.
The secular nature of the ghazal, its dissemination through

the popular press, film songs, the schools of singing and the long, late-night sessions of mushairas, or poetry readings, where it is both recited and sung, have helped it reach a cross-section of the masses. This argument is well supported by the fact that individual shers of well-known ghazals have acquired epigrammatic value and have become a part of the common memory of both the ordinary and the educated people. These shers have remarkably supplemented their serious discourses and ordinary exchanges of ideas. To put it simply, if there is a situation, there is a sher to score a point in argument, or to earn the appreciation of the addressee. The ghazal has thus been a harbinger of a culture where the poets have emerged as social icons and their readers and listeners as figures of cultivated manners.

Even though the ghazal has been immensely popular with poets, readers and a variety of audiences, it has also been subjected to severe criticism. There is a view that it offends healthy minds as it thrives on unbridled imagination and creates only disunities. It has, therefore, been asserted that it is a semi-savage form of poetry where the poet roams in the realms of fancy and takes the reader far away from reality. Others, who hold the opposite view, defend it exactly for what the purists choose to malign it. They argue that the worth of the ghazal lies greatly in its disunities and its free associations of ideas. They assert, therefore, that each sher of a ghazal is a climax unto itself and all the shers put together emerge as a series of climaxes. They argue that each sher is an independent unit of a poem, and that each sher tests the imaginative virility of both the poet and the reader. The fact that the best of the poets have invariably expressed themselves through the medium of ghazal, and that it is in the ghazals that the biggest capital of Urdu poetry lies invested, goes to establish its unquestionable significance. Moving beyond this controversy, it is important to note that apart from representing the broader human condition, the ghazal represents a certain cultural condition. It reflects the basic human urge to locate the truth within the truth and it connects with the reader or listener more intimately than any other literary form. The history of its origin and development in various sites of the East and the West bear it out quite amply.

Context

The ghazal is a literary curiosity. Its contexts are many and they are traceable broadly in the domains of language, cultural historiography, socio-political history, comparative studies and critical reception. It is, first, in the context of language that the ghazal must be assessed. Considering that the great tradition of this inimitable literary form is to be found primarily in the Eastern languages, more especially Arabic, Persian and Urdu, one may safely assert that it has something to do with the genius of these languages. Further, it is also concerned with the literary sensibility that these languages have nourished over the ages. This sensibility has called for cultivating and pruning a certain form and employing certain literary devices that are special to these languages, as are the images and metaphors, symbols and myths, wit and humour that they execute. Ultimately, they together constitute a literary culture and identify a people for their literary taste and heritage. With the passage that a language follows in the course of its development, it creates literary texts of varying degrees. In this process, a language sustains its heritage and reaches out to newer configurations. Like every other language, the Urdu language has also followed this principle. In spite of its unsteady survival in its own habitats and the complex linguistic politicking in India, the Urdu language has shown remarkable perseverance. It has negotiated with all the odds and lived on with its identified readership as an enduring language. The ghazal, being the most popular of all the literary forms in the Urdu language, offers a curious case study with relation to language, linguistic mapping and the politics of literary production and consumption.

The second context of the ghazal lies in cultural historiography. This may be done in terms of locating the individual poets, periods and poetic practices in a cultural matrix. The ghazal as a cultural sign may be assessed through its particular form and its various genres like the romantic, the mystical, the philosophical, the ironic, the mundane and the innumerable others. All cultural histories written in terms of chronology and ages, individual icons and art forms, ideological preoccupations and stylistic formations, beliefs and practices, must take the literary life of a language and their people into consideration for a broader understanding of a larger cultural condition. The ghazal, being the most primordial way of poetic expression, holds a distinct position in this scheme of reading. Considered in this perspective, it is likely to authenticate the long-preserved reputation of this art-form in a larger framework of cultural iconography. A cultural mapping of art-forms, with the ghazal as an example, may help determine its value even among those who are not directly exposed to this language but have come to enjoy its riches only through popular cultural agencies like the musical soirees where a ghazal is sung, or a mushaira where it is heartily recited, or a public platform where it is creatively performed.

The socio-political histories of the lands and the people where the ghazal found its acceptance should be the third context for our consideration. Apart from meeting several other aims, history in its simplest term also catalogues people as addresses, receivers or beneficiaries of political dispensations and socio-cultural boons and banes. Literature, in turn, and to be specific, the ghazal in its own way, has chronicled them all. It has created its own metaphors of acceptance or denial. While it has reiterated its stock metaphors, it has also created metaphors of difference by which it has acquired its resilience. Since the socio-political context is an important mainstay of modern knowledge, one of its sources lies in the life of the ghazal as much as it lies in the life of the people it has addressed. The ghazal in its socio-political context is a forte not much explored, although so worth exploring, in terms of the identity of people, places and their essential predicaments.

The fourth context of the ghazal lies in comparative studies. We may discover its worth in comparison with other literary forms and genres and their attendant advantages and compulsions. This makes way further for studying the phenomenon of impact and response at the levels of form, genre, language and style. It provides a way to study the texts and tropes, cultural milieu, and prescriptive or oppositional discourses at multiple levels. This might happen within a homogenous or even an alien cultural site. Living literary forms are not sacrosanct and if they remain so, they grow effete in their splendid isolation, which the ghazal has denied throughout its history of birth, growth and development. It has been remarkable for broadening its frontiers by incorporating a range of literary and related references. The comparative studies that call for the determination of a text in relation to other languages, literary cultures, residual, dominant or emergent fields of reference, thematic and generic intermixing, inherited and invented interplay of texts, could locate the ghazal in a larger framework of reading. It could, thus, impart the ghazal its larger relevance and demonstrate, in turn, its greater meaningfulness.

The fifth context of the ghazal may be found in its critical reception. It may be read in semiotic terms in relation to archetypes, signs and symbols. This would afford an understanding of the basic references that a text creates around itself. The possible intents of the ghazal may also be explored in psychoanalytical terms to which it lends itself quite easily with reference to the real, the imaginary and the symbolic. Yet another interesting way of reading the ghazal could be found in the feminist method by examining the elements of jouissance, patriarchy and phallocentrism, or even the queer practice of referring to the issues related to sexuality, gender and identity. A literary text in our times that has already lent itself for adoption in larger geographical and linguistic areas may be read quite appropriately in a post-colonial way with reference to its hybridity, alterity and difference. It would be rewarding, in this manner, to examine it as a liberal form of art that is historically and culturally situated. Politics of interpretations and dissident readings in relation to cultural materialism, as also the phenomenological reduction, being the hallmarks of our current reading practices, may bring the ghazal to a newer field of interpretation. The ghazal is multifaceted in its merits and it rightly qualifies for multifaceted readings.

The ghazal is on the move. It has many languages to speak in and many sites to belong to. It has been discovering and refurbishing itself in all its sites. With a history of more than five centuries in India, it also tells the story of the development of Urdu as a language of literary expression and its centres of writing and reading. In its modern form, it has obliterated the distinction between the poetic and the non-poetic, the formal and the non-formal, and has gone beyond the spatial confines of a given location or centre. The ghazal is now being written in Hindi, Punjabi, Gujarati, Marathi and Kashmiri. It is now providing new contexts of writing and reading, of linguistic liberalism, literary historiography, socio-political historicizing and critical reading. Since the Partition of India, the ghazal has flourished with remarkable linguistic vitality and thematic variety in Pakistan. Of all the languages in which it developed and matured, Urdu has proved to be the most enduring, in addition to Persian, in which it has been claiming and reclaiming itself and acquiring new terms of stylistic and thematic references.

Anisur Rahman

METAPHYSICAL BEGINNINGS

An early avatar of what came to be known as Urdu in the late eighteenth century is traceable in the works of Amir Khusrau, way back in the late thirteenth century. However, literary history records the beginnings of Urdu poetry since the Deccan rulers of Golconda that had emerged as an independent state with the decline of the Bahmani Sultanate in 1527. The two most significant of the Deccan poets—Mohammad Quli Qutub Shah and Vali Deccani—initiated the great tradition of Urdu poetry that flowered in various parts of northern India later.

Although the Mughal Empire had started declining by the end of the seventeenth century, Persian remained the language of the court, the nobility and the poets. Poetry in the new-fangled and so-called Urdu language was still in its infancy but it was vying for a place alongside the poetry written in the canonical Persian. As a language that grew out of the military camp, Urdu had closely drawn upon other languages like Arabic, Persian, Turkish and Braj, and had come to be known variously at various points of time as Deccani, Gujari, Hindi/Hindavi, Dehlavi, Rekhta and Urdu-i Mu'alla. While Mohammad Quli Qutub Shah and Vali Decanni wrote in Decanni Urdu, Mirza Mazhar Jan-e Janan wrote in Dehlavi Urdu. Although Jan-e Janan's chosen language of poetic expression was Persian, he got inclined towards writing in Urdu as he was impressed by Vali's linguistic innovations and saw the possibility of evolving it as a new language with great literary potential.

Poetry in the Deccan had a rich variety of sources to draw upon: it reflected the communal harmony of the land, represented its flora and fauna, absorbed the linguistic habits of its folk and recorded literartures, and finally, negotiated with the Persian influences without being unduly swayed by it. As opposed to this, poetry in the northern parts of India had a different set of conditions to fall back upon: it reflected the cultural norms defined by the continuity of Muslim rule, its court and nobility, refinement and elitism, as also the unitary dominance of the Persian literary culture. The poetry of Mohammad Quli Qutub Shah, Vali Deccani and Mirza Mazhar Jan-e Janan had a certain metaphysical aura about it which was preserved further by other poets of the south and the north. While Ashraf Bayabani, Hasan Shauqi, Mohammad Qutub Shah, Abdullah Qutub Shah, Mulla Asadullah Wajhi, Ibne Nishati and Mohammad Nusrat Nusrati represented the Deccan sensibility, Sirajuddin Ali Khan Arzoo, Najmuddin Abru, Mohammad Shakir Naji, Sheikh Sharfuddin Mazmoon, Zahuruddin Hatim and Sadruddin Mohammad Khan Fayez represented the northern sensibility.

I

Mohammad Quli Qutub Shah

Mohammad Quli Qutub Shah (1565?–1611?), popularly known and recorded in history as Abul Muzaffar Mohammad Quli Qutub Shah and Sultan Mohammad Quli Qutub Shah, was the fifth ruler of the Qutub Shahi dynasty of Golconda and the founder of the city of Hyderabad. He was born in Golconda, Hyderabad (there is no unanimity about the dates of his birth and death). The legend goes that he founded a city called Bhag Nagar after one of his beloveds, Bhagmati. Bhag Nagar later became Hyderabad once Bhagmati was renamed Hyder Mahal. He is said to have erected other monuments in the name of his other twelve beloveds, and he celebrated his romance with them in his poetry separately.

Shah who wrote in Persian, Telugu and Deccani—a variant of Urdu—is justifiably the first poet in Deccani Urdu with at least fifty thousand shers to his credit put together in his *Kulliyaat*. Acclaimed to be a major voice, he practised all poetic forms. He wrote on a variety of issues concerning communal

life and the sentiments of the common man, their festivals and
faiths, love and the pleasures of union, in a frank and disarming
manner. Drawing upon Hindu culture, as also upon the Persian
culture and its literary tradition, he developed a secular view of
love, life and literature. A contemporary of Tulsidas, he blended
the best traditions of the two streams of thought and life to
impart a new halo to his poetry. His poetic merit lies in his
simplicity and musicality which he appropriated to project an
inclusive view of life and art. Essentially a poet of Deccan flora
and fauna, Shah was a kind-hearted ruler, a passionate lover
and a great patron of fine arts and architecture.

I

Piyaa baaj pyaala piyaa jaaye naa
Piyaa baaj yek til jiyaa jaaye naa

Kaheethey piyaa bin saboori karoon
Kahhiya jaaye amma kiyaa jaaye naa

Naheen ishq jis wo badaa kood hai
Kadhein us se mil biseeyaa jaaye naa

Qutub Shah na de mujh diwaane ku pand
Diwaane ku kuchh pand diyaa jaaye naa

I

I can't ever drink my drink without my love
I can't ever breathe; I sink without my love

I should be patient, you say, without my love
How unfair! I can't even blink without my love

A boor indeed is one who can't be in love
I'm no boor; I'm on the brink without my love

No counsels, Qutub Shah, none to this crazy one
I'm the one; I can't even think without my love

2

Kahiyaa ke bosa seti haman too jawaan karo
Kahiye ke prit ki baat taman jiu ka jaan karo

Kahiyaa ke aaftaab kiran aayi qaul koon
Kahiye ke qaul jot soon likh kar rawaan karo

Kahiyaa adhar tumhare jiu koon jalaawate
Hans kar kahi ye baat nako tum bayaan karo

Kahiyaa ke haq parasti karo but pujan sato
Kahiye ke donon baat mein ek imtihaan karo

Kahiyaa ke aadmi ka murawwat naheen taman
Kahiye ke bus hai ishq tumhara nihaan karo

Kahiyaa ke aashiqan koon dukhaane ka bhed kya
Kahiye ke aashiqi mane goongee zabaan karo

Kahiyaa ke mad gulaabi jalaadewe jeeu koon
Kahiye azal se must hoon tum naasamaan karo

Kahiyaa ke marhamat ki nazar soon nawaaz mujh
Kahiye hamaari panth mane jaanfishaan karo

Kahiyaa tumhaari sewaa Ma'ani ka daulat hai
Kahiye ke tum bhi sewaa baraabar shahaan karo

2

Make me young with a kiss, my love, I said
If it's love, breathe life into breath, she said

The sun has shown, rays say their say, I said
If words be rays, write the rays and send, she said

Look, your delicate lips sear my heart, I said
She giggled in jest; don't tell me that, she said

Bow down to the real God, not an image, I said
Then why don't you test me in both, she said

You don't respect a man, you don't, I said
You don't know what love, hide your love, she said

Why put your love in pain, why so, I said
If in love, seal your lips, my love, she said

That pink wine sears my heart, my breath, I said
Well, I'm myself drunk since eternity, she said

Be kind to me, do me a favour, I said
Then shed your life for that very love, she said

Being at your feet is all that I cherish, my love
Then you should better serve the lords, not me, she said

2

Vali Deccani

Vali Deccani (1667?–1707?) whose name is variously recorded in history as Shamsuddin Mohammad Vali, Shams Valiullah, Valiuddin Vali and Vali Mohammad Vali, is generally recognized in literary history as Vali Deccani and, at times, Vali Gujarati. The accounts of his place and dates of birth and death remain unconfirmed. Said to have been born in Ahmedabad, Gujarat, or Aurangabad, Maharashtra, he travelled to the far ends of the south and the north, including Delhi. He lies buried in the city of Ahmedabad where his grave was vandalized during the infamous riots of 2002.

Vali lived in a time of political and social turmoil but sought his intellectual sustenance from the larger mystic traditions of India. He considered literature as a way of negotiating between the physical and the spiritual. The figure of the lover in his poetry represents both the worlds of the sensual and the non-sensual. Even though well versed in the Persian literary tradition and Deccani and Hindi phraseology, Vali surprised the literary circle in Delhi with his non-Persianized Urdu divaan and its linguistic freshness, which till then was called rekhta, a language of the lesser literary kind, not quite fit for sober poetic expression. His choice for the plebeian idiom and his effort to blend it with other linguistic and literary traditions of the north and the south altered the stereotypical notions of those who championed the purity of language as a necessary condition for serious literary expression. A master image-maker and an innovator of refreshing similes and metaphors, Vali has come to be categorized as a canonical figure in Urdu poetry.

I

Ab judaayi na kar Khuda soon dar
Bewafaayi na kar Khuda soon dar

Mat taghaaful ko raah de ai shokh
Jag hansaayi na kar Khuda soon dar

Hai judaayi mein zindagi mushkil
Aa judaayi na kar Khuda soon dar

Aashiqaan koon shaheed kar ke sanam
Kaf hinaayi na kar Khuda soon dar

Aarsi dekh kar na ho maghroor
Khudnumaayi na kar Khuda soon dar

Us soon jo aashnaa-i daar naheen
Aashnaayi na kar Khuda soon dar

Rang-e aashiq ghazab soon ai zaalim
Kuhr baayi na kar Khuda soon dar

Ai Vali ghair-e aastaana-i yaar
Juba saayi na kar Khuda soon dar

I

Don't part with me for now, fear God
Don't break my love your vow, fear God

Don't turn your face, my playful love!
Don't let them raise eyebrows, fear God

Life, in parting, is tough indeed
Don't part, don't disavow, fear God

Don't slay your love, don't shed his blood
Don't smear your hand for now, fear God

Don't see the mirror, don't be so proud
Don't brag, don't paint your brow, fear God

He knows not what gallows, what gibbet
Don't kiss his hand or brow, fear God

Strange are the ways of love for sure
Don't shock my love for now, fear God

Don't bow to a friend or foe, don't you
Restrain, O Vali! Don't bow, fear God

2

Kiyaa mujh ishq koon zaalim ne aab aahista aahista
Ke aatish gul koon karti hai gulaab aahista aahista

Wafadaari ne dilbar ki bujhaayaa aatish-e ghum koon
Ke garmi daf'a karta hai gulaab aahista aahista

Ajab kuchh lutf rakhta hai shab-e khalwat mein gul roo soon
Khitaab aahista aahista jawaab aahista aahista

Mere dil koon kiya bekhud teri ankhiyaan ne aakhir koon
Ke jiun behosh karti hai sharaab aahista aahista

Hua tujh ishq soon ai aatesheen roo dil mera paani
Ke jiun galtaa hai aatish soon gulaab aahista aahista

Adaa-o naaz soon aataa hai wo raushan jabeen ghar soon
Ke jiun mashriq se nikle aaftaab aahista aahista

Vali mujh dil mein aataa hai khayaal-e yaar-e beparwaa
Ke jiun ankhiyaan manein aataa hai khwaab aahista aahista

2

I was all aflame in love; she won my heart bit by bit
Just as the flame makes a bud bloom, bit by bit

My love is surely kind; she quelled my flaming fire of grief
Just as the flaming rose cools the searing heat, bit by bit

It's a rare delight to speak with love on a quiet night
Seek a reply hint by hint; send a reply, sigh by sigh

Your glance, at last, made my impatient heart lose control
Just as the wine makes one lose all control, sip by sip

Your blazing face has won my heart for good, my dear love!
Just as a rose softens like fire, petal by petal

My love walks out with a radiant face and charming grace
Just as the glowing sun shows up from the East, ray by ray

Vali, the thought of your careless love draws you now to her
Just as sweet dreams draw to dreamer's eye, image by image

3

Mirza Mazhar Jan-e Janan

Mirza Mazhar Jan-e Janan (1698?–1781), also known by his title, Shamsuddin Habibullah, was born in Agra according to one source, and in Kalabagh in Malwa, according to another. His father had migrated from Deccan to Agra, where Jan-e Janan received his early education before his father came to Delhi and was rewarded with a high position by Emperor Aurangzeb. Jan-e Janan inherited from his father the taste for a life of Sufistic leanings, which he carried to the greatest heights and emerged as a major Sufi of the Naqshbandi order. He had a large number of disciples who venerated him for his incomparable merit as a Sufi and a poet. He commanded equal respect among those in the royalty and the nobility. Shah Waliullah, the great Islamic scholar of his time, held him in very high seteem for his rare understanding of Islam and the traditions of the Prophet. Sources testify that on account of a difference in matters of religious faith and his unreserved expression of his conviction, he was brutally attacked and killed by a fanatic. He lies buried in Delhi but only those would know who recognize his spiritual and literary worth.

Jan-e Janan came to be acknowledged as a major poet in both Persian and Urdu, although the volume of his work in Urdu is far less than in Persian. He privileged the Persian modes of expression and made way for the enrichment of Urdu as a literary language. He did not pay much attention to the art and artifice of poetry but chose a natural and direct mode of expression. As he brought the refinement of Persian to Urdu poetry, he chose to reject the oblique and the obscure in thought and language, bringing poetry close to natural human perception and understanding. His idiom echoed the contemporary idiom of his location but it also harked back to the Deccani dialect. Jan-e Janan has left behind a Persian divaan called *Divaan-e Mazhar*, three collections of his letters, and an anthology of select poetry from classical Persian masters called *Khairat-e Jawaahir*.

I

Ye dil kab ishq ke qaabil rahaa hai
Kahaan humko dimaagh-o dil rahaa hai

Naheen aataa kisee takiye ooper khwaab
Ye sar paaon se tere hil rahaa hai

Khuda ke waaste us ko na toko
Yehi ek shahr mein qaatil rahaa hai

Dil-o deen se toh guzre ab tera ghar
Naheen maloon ko manzil rahaa hai

Ghanimat jaan qaatil jaan-e Mazhar
Ye maqtoolon mein tuk bismil rahaa hai

Na uthhnaa ghar se Mazhar ka na jaaye
Koee milne ke kab qaabil rahaa hai

I

This poor heart never deserved your kind love, none
I didn't have the head or heart for your love, none

No dreams visit my pillow, no delusions, none
Only your feet touch my head, never your dreams, none

Don't bother him, for God's sake, don't ever bother
That is the only love left in town, none else, none

I have crossed over both life and faith, and now
I am at your threshold; I know no other, none

It's God's will, O assassin, that Mazhar alone
Writhes and wriggles, as he does, none else none

Mazhar doesn't move; he doesn't ever leave his abode
No good now, he is no good; none can see him, none

2

Gul ko jo gul kahoon to tere roo ko kyaa kahoon
Dar ko jo dar kahoon to us aansoon ko kyaa kahoon

Mujh per huaa hai tang sajan arsa-i sukhan
Boloon nigah ko tegh to abroo ko kyaa kahoon

Muddat se us khayaal ke aaya hoon beech mein
Gar moo kahoon kamar ko toh gesoo ko kyaa kahoon

Rone se tujh firaaq ke aankhein meri gayein
Dubaa ye khaandaan us aansoon ko kyaa kahoon

Diwaana kar liya hai meri jaan-o tan ke tayein
Maali teri bahaar ke jaadu ko kyaa kahoon

Kartaa hai jaur jo ewaz apne hi yaar ke
Mazhar tere sitamgar-e badkhoo ko kyaa kahoon

2

If I call the blossom a blossom, what shall I call your face?
If I call the fear a fear, what shall I call your tears?

The realm of words is vast indeed; it has now shrunk on me
If I call your looks a sword, what shall I call your curly brows?

I have long tried to find a name, I have never got one
If I call your waist curling hair, what shall I call your tresses?

I have shed tears in parting; I have lost my vision, Love!
When my world is drowned and gone, what shall I call my tears?

It's both my body and my soul that go to you in your praise
O Gardener! What shall I call the magic of your spring?

He who chooses to oppress none else, only his dear friends
Tell me, Mazhar! What shall I call this unfair friend of yours?

TOWARDS ENLIGHTENMENT

The eighteenth century in Urdu poetry, generally identified with Mirza Mohammad Rafi Sauda and Mir Taqi Mir, marked the beginnings of a golden period. It made remarkable strides in two directions: first, it refined and enriched Urdu as a language of poetry; and second, it cultivated poetry as a precious art that evolved with a great care for craftsmanship. This age saw the emergence of Urdu as a virile medium of poetic expression in several parts of northern India. Following the tradition laid down by the three major poets—Mohammad Quli Qutub Shah and Vali Deccani in the Deccan, and Mirza Mazhar Jan-e Janan in Delhi—poets like Mirza Mohammad Rafi Sauda, Mir Taqi Mir, Siraj Aurangabadi and Khwaja Mir Dard, along with Mir Soze and Qayam Chandpuri, empowered Urdu as a language of poetry, which so far had been dominated by Persian. They showed clear signs of mature literary imagination with their unique ability to evolve and situate their new-found metaphors and symbols in newer linguistic configurations. Even while they drew upon the Persian literary stock, they distinguished themselves by making individual interventions at the level of language and disengaging from deliberate attempts at writing allusive verse. The ghazal of this age was, thus, able to redefine the idea of love and the figure of the beloved, both in secular and spiritual terms. Importantly enough, while these poets worked towards the evolution of ghazal as a popular form, they also moved towards developing other forms of poetry after the Persian models, like *qasida* (panegyric), *marsiya* (elegy), *mathnawi* (rhymed narratives) and *hajwa* (lampoon), and laid the foundations of what became the canonical forms of poetry in the ages to come.

The poetry of this age, characterized by a move towards the age of enlightenment, expressed a sense of acute emotional and physical dislocations which was borne by the poets in their bid to reconcile with their times. Their discontent was born out of the conditions that contemporary history brought forth in terms of conflicts, invasions, battles and acquisition of political power ever since the death of Aurangzeb in 1707. The poets lamented in metaphoric and symbolic ways the fallout of what in physical terms may be identified as the invasion of Nadir Shah (1738–39), the seven expeditions of Ahmad Shah Abdali (1748–67), the Maratha expansionist activities following the death of Aurangzeb in 1707, the arrival of Warren Hastings as the first Governor-General of India (1773), and the attack by Rohilla chieftain Ghulam Qadir (1788), all of which have stayed on as the terms of reference of eighteenth-century India.

4

Mirza Mohammad Rafi Sauda

Mirza Mohammad Rafi Sauda (1713?–1781), son of an aristocrat father who had migrated from Kabul to India for trade, was born in Delhi. He was well provided for to meet the needs of a decent life and lived in comfort. Not attracted by the mercantile interests of his family, Sauda nursed his passion as a poet under the patronage of poet Shah Hatim. Although he received patronage at the Mughal court, he took umbrage against the royal whims. He chose to leave Delhi when the city fell prey to Maratha attacks after the death of Aurangzeb and went to several places in Uttar Pradesh. At the ripe age of sixty, he arrived in Lucknow where Nawab Asifuddaulah patronized and rewarded him with an annual stipend of rupees six thousand.

Sauda wrote in Persian before coming to Urdu and expressed his maturity of thought and linguistic finesse in both languages. John Borthwick Gilchrist (1759–1841), the famous linguist and Indologist, acknowledged rather profusely that he learnt his Urdu from Sauda's divaan. The Persian literary tradition helped him acquire a tone and tenor which he adopted to his benefit for his poetry in Urdu. He looked at life sportingly, enjoyed his vigour and optimism and relished the pleasures of life in full measure. His ghazals hold close to the tone and tenor of panegyric which he brought to its height. Marked for his vitality of imagination, precise turns of phrases and compact expressions, he practised various forms of poetry like panegyric, satire and elegy, and emerged as one of the canonical poets in Urdu. His works have been put together in several *divaans* and *kulliyaat*.

I

Naseem hai tere kuche main aur sabaa bhi hai
Hamaari khaak se tuk dekh kuchh rahaa bhi hai

Tera ghuroor mera ijz taa kuja zaalim
Har ek baat ki aakhir kuchh intihaa bhi hai

Jale hai shamma se parwaana aur main tujh se
Kaheen hai mehr bhi jag mein kaheen wafaa bhi hai

Khayaal apne mein go hoon taraana sanjaan mast
Karaahne ke dilon ko kabhi sunaa bhi hai

Zabaan-e shikwa siwaa ab zamaana mein haihaat
Koee kiso se baham deegar aashnaa bhi hai

Sitam rawaa hai aseeron pe is qadar sayyaad
Chaman chaman kaheen bulbul ki ab nawaa bhi hai

Sambhal ke rakhyo qadam dasht-e khaar mein majnoon
Ke is nawaah mein Sauda barahna paa bhi hai

I

A fine breeze blows there, gentle draughts glide too
But does your lane bear my ashes' pride too?

How long your pride, how long my modesty!
Isn't there, my love, an end to your pride too?

The flame burns the moth; I burn in your flame
Why doesn't the world look at the lover's side too?

Engrossed in my thoughts, I sing my own song
Did you ever hear how my heart cried too?

Why complain, why bother, it's all long gone
Is there someone to get in love's stride too?

Why this caging of free birds, O hunter!
Can't you hear the bulbul's note, can that hide too?

Take care, wild lover, in this desert of thorns
Sauda, barefoot stands by the wayside too

2

Jo guzri mujh pe mat us se kaho hua so hua
Balaa kashaan-e-mohabbat pe jo hua so hua

Mubaada ho koee zaalim tera garebaan geer
Mere lahoo ko to daaman se dho hua so hua

Pahunch chukaa hai sir-e zakhm dil talak yaaro
Koee siyo koee maraham dharo hua so hua

Kahe hai sun ke meri sarguzasht wo berahm
Ye kaun zikr hai jaane bhi do hua so hua

Khuda ke waaste aa darguzar gunah se mere
Na hoga phir kabho ai tund khoo hua so hua

Ye kaun haal hai ahvaal-e dil pe ai aankho
Na phoot phoot ke itnaa baho hua so hua

Diyaa use dil-o deen ab ye jaan hai Sauda
Phir aage dekhiye jo ho so ho, hua so hua

2

Don't mention what befell me; whatever happened, happened
To the love-stricken one; whatever happened, happened

Lest a tyrant hold you guilty for not a fault, my friend
Just wash my blood from your garb; whatever happened,
happened

My wound has found a way, has reached the heart, my
friends, at last
Sew up the wound, put a balm; whatever happened, happened

That heartless one tells me on hearing my tale of woe
What a story to bring up now; whatever happened, happened

For God's sake, just pardon me my sins, O fretful one!
It won't ever happen again; whatever happened, happened

What is this, why do you cry on the demise of dear heart
Don't shed tears; whatever happened, happened

I gave my heart and faith to her, now I give my life Sauda
Just see what happens now; forget whatever happened, happened

5

Siraj Aurangabadi

Siraj Aurangabadi (1715-1763) is the popular name of Syed Sirajuddin. He was born in Aurangabad, Maharashtra, a place named after the Mughal Emperor Aurangzeb. An embodiment of uncontrollable passion and impatience with the world around him from the very early years of his life, Siraj turned into a dervish. He abandoned home, wandered in the wilderness, wrote verse, and had to be brought back home in a tattered condition. He had to be kept under strict watch for several years until he achieved a semblance of normalcy and transformed into a Sufi, acquiring a high status in the realm of mysticism.

In the early years, Siraj, the impetuous soul, began by writing verse in Persian during his frequent bouts of deviation from the normal ways of life. He also wrote in Urdu with equal felicity. He composed his verse feverishly and lost much of it, as one overpowered by the raptures of imagination would often do. He would soon complete his divaan of over five thousand shers.

Apart from the ghazal, Siraj also practised other forms of poetry, including the long narrative forms like *mathnawi* and *qasida*. After the decline of the Deccan kingdoms, when Aurangabad became the literary centre, Siraj emerged as a major link between the old and the new styles of the Deccan school of poetry. Divine love is the central concern of his poetry and he spent all his life trying to unravel the mysteries of divinity in direct and metaphorical terms. His divaan represents his metaphysical concerns and mystical preoccupations that arose from his awareness of the physical and the transcendental, the secular and the religious. His poetry is a way of primeval engagement with the self, executed with rare lyric grace.

I

Tumhaari zulf ka har taar Mohan
Hua mere gale ka haar Mohan

Tasawwur kar tera husn-e araq naak
Meri aankhein hain gauhar baar Mohan

Dam-e aakhir talak hoon kaafir-e ishq
Hua taar-e nafas zunnaar Mohan

Birah ka jaan kundan hai nimat sakht
Dikha us waqt per deedaar Mohan

Hamaare mushaf-e dil ki qasam kha
Kiyaa hai zulm ka inkaar Mohan

Gul-e aariz koon tere yaad kar kar
Hua hai dil mera gulzaar Mohan

Siraj aatish mein hai tere firaaqon
Bujha sa mehr seen ek baar Mohan

I

Of your lock, each hair, O Mohan
Like a garland, I wear, O Mohan

I think of your fluid beauty
Teardrops roll to sear, O Mohan

Till my end, I'm a lover, no less
My breath a Brahmin's thread-wear, O Mohan

Parting is pure gold, hard to grip
Just come, I'm in despair, O Mohan

I swear by the book of my heart
When worries ensnare, O Mohan

Remembering your blossom-cheeks
My heart sees spring fair, O Mohan

Siraj is all aflame in parting
Be kind, hear his prayer, O Mohan

2

Jaan-o dil seen main giraftaar hoon kin ka un ka
Banda-i-be zar-o deenaar hoon kin ka un ka

Sabr ke bagh ke mandwe se jhadaa jiun phool
Ab to laachaar gale haar hoon kin ka un ka

Hauz-e kausar ki naheen chaah zakhandaan ki qasam
Tashna-i sharbat-e deedaar hoon kin ka un ka

Lab-o rukhsaar ke gul qand seen laazim hai ilaaj
Dil ke aazaar mein beemaar hoon kin ka un ka

Muudatein huin ke hua khaana-i zanjeer kharaab
Basta-i zulf-e girah daar hoon kin ka un ka

Tashna-i-marg koon hai aab-e suraahi dam-e tegh
Bismil-e abru-i khamdaar hoon kin ka un ka

Naahaq us sang dilee mein mujhe dete hain shikast
Main toh aaeena-i sarkaar hoon kin ka un ka

Gulshan-e wasl main rahtaa hoon ghazal khwan-e firaaq
Andaleeb-e gul-e rukhsaar hoon kin ka un ka

Main kahaa rahm patangon pe kar ai jaan-e Siraj
Tab kaha shamm-e shab-e taar hoon kin ka un ka

2

I'm a prisoner by heart and soul—of whom? Only him
A worthless being of no riches—of whom? Only him

Like a flower fallen from the bower of patience
Now I'm a helpless garland—for whom? Only him

I don't wish for the river of paradise, I swear
I only crave for a kind look—of whom? Only him

Only a fare of a fair face may bring me cure
I'm sick of heart, O my heart—for whom? Only him

Ages have gone by since the house of chains was ruined
I'm chained to the locks of love—of whom? Only him

For one close to death, a wine drop is a dagger's slash
I'm slain by the eyebrows—of whom? Only him

What's defeat, I don't compete with the hard-hearted
I'm only the mirror of love—of whom? Only him

In the grove of union, I sing a dirge of our parting
I'm a bird of the blossom-cheeks—of whom? Only him

I said, be kind to the helpless moths, O Siraj
Then said: I'm a lamp in night's gloom—of whom? Only him

6

Khwaja Mir Dard

Khwaja Mir Dard (1721–1785), a descendant of respected Sufi migrants from Bukhara to India, was born in Delhi where he spent all his life, despite the invasions of Nadir Shah and Ahmed Shah Abdali, as also the Maratha conquest of north-west India. Keenly interested in music, both vocal and instrumental, he mastered his art to perfection and also hosted soirees of music. As a Sufi, he was respected equally by the royalty and the nobility, but bothered little about their praise and plaudits. This Sufi poet and theologian of eighteenth-century Delhi is an important representative of the Naqshbandi-Mujaddidi lineage of Sufism. He also became the leader and theoretician of the Muhammadi path and fashioned himself in the image of the Prophet Muhammad, appointed by God as His messenger on the earth.

Dard had mastery over the Arabic, Persian and Urdu languages. His close reading of the Holy Qur'an, Traditions of the Prophet, jurisprudence, and religious literature defined the nature of his poetry. His expertise in music further defined his assured tone and tenor in poetic expression. Effortless in his expression and direct in his addresses, he emerged as a renowned mystic poet, both in Persian and Urdu. He is, by turn, an impassioned advocate for poetry and humble apologist for art. He considered poetry as a gift among the many other gifts of God to mankind. Poetry, to him, was an inspired speech addressed both to the human and the divine. He differentiated between two types of speech, or *kalaam*: one of them being internal, or *nafsi*, and the other being verbal, or *lafzi*. He believed that a poet negotiates between two types of speech: the external, or *zaahiri;* and internal, or *baatini*. This reflection on language, speech and expression underlines the modes of Dard's poetic apprehension and expression. He has to his credit a collection of Urdu ghazals, a Persian divaan, a prose discourse called *Ilm-ul Kitaab*, a collection of mystical sayings called *Chahaar Risaala*, and a book on the Muhammadi path of Sufism.

I

Tohmatein chand apne zimme dhar chale
Jis liye aai the so ham kar chale

Zindagi hai ya koee toofan hai
Hum to is jeene ke haathon mar chale

Kya hamein kaam in gulon se ai sabaa
Aik dum aai idhar, oodhar chale

Dosto dekha tamaasha yaan ka sab
Tum raho khush hum to apne ghar chale

Shamma ki maanind hum is bazm mein
Chashm-e tar aai the, daaman tar chale

Dhoondte hain aap se us ko pare
Sheikh sahib chhod ghar, baahar chale

Hum na jaane paai baahar aap se
Wo hi aage aa gaya jeedhar chale

Hum jahaan mein aai the tanhaa wale
Saath apne ab use le kar chale

Saaqiyaa yaan lag rahaa hai chal chalaao
Jab talak bus chal sake saaghar chale

Dard kuchh maloom hai ye log sub
Kis taraf se aai the keedhar chale

I

I put on myself many a blame, before I left
I only did for what I came, before I left

Is this a life, or a rough storm I suffer?
In life's term, I was life's claim, before I left

Gentle breeze! What's my business with blossoms?
I left in a flash, as I came, before I left

I watched all the games of this place, dear friends
Let me bless you all the same, before I left

I lived here like a lamp, as long as I lived
With tears I came but earned shame, before I left

Poor priest looks for him beyond himself
He left his home for a new aim, before I left

I couldn't ever go beyond you, but only you
Crossed my path only to claim, before I left

I had come to this world alone, nothing in hand
I carried the world, all the same, before I left

Saqi! This is the time to leave, hurry up please
Fill my cup, let me drink, be aflame, before I left

Dard! Can you tell me, who we are—you and me?
From where I came, what's my aim, before I left?

2

Jam'a mein afraad-e aalam ek hain
Gul ke sab auraaq-e barham ek hain

Howe kab wahdat mein kasrat se khalal
Jism-o jaan go do hain per hum ek hain

Nau-e insaan ki buzurgi se tuk ek
Hazarat-e Jibreel mahram ek hain

Daal hai us per hi Qur'an ka nuzool
Baat ki fehmeed main hum ek hain

Muttafiq aapas main hain ahl-e shuhood
Dard aankhein dekh baaham ek hain

2

In all, all the beings of the world are really one
Petals are so many, but the flower is really one

How can this medley ever disrupt unity
Body and soul are two, the two are really one

Of mankind's supremacy over all others
That's a truth Gabriel knows; the truth is really one

Qur'an's revelation is a sure proof of this:
In getting the truth, we all are really one

All the believers surely agree with each other
Dard, the eyes are two but the two are really one

7

Mir Taqi Mir

Mir Taqi Mir (1723–1810) is the nom de plume of Mohammad Taqi, who was born in Agra of a Sufi father. Mir's father advised him to adopt the way of *ishq*, or love as a way of life. Mir migrated to Delhi, already ravaged by chaotic events, for a living after his father's death, where he would meet his ends with difficulty even though he received some patronage from the nobility. Trying to find his patronage and source of sustenance, a proud Mir kept moving from one court or nobility to another for twenty-five years. It was at the ripe age of sixty that he reached Nawab Asifuddaulah in Lucknow; where he lived till his death with the memories of Delhi as a lost home. Mir lived in a period of great political crisis. Both the literary centres had failed him and he spent his life wondering if there would ever be a resolution for him. It is reported that his grave in Lucknow is untraceable as a rail line has been laid over the spot.

Mir's philosophical reflections on his personal despair and disappointments imparted a unique strength to his poetry. He expressed himself in a language which was still in the early stages of its growth and development and had not been strengthened by a studied literary tradition. His poetry makes immense promises for the representation of the broader manifestations of life and the world. Generally supposed to be a poet of pain and of pining, Mir initiated the reader to an understanding of the larger realities of life. He expressed himself best in the ghazal form but he has also left behind narrative poems and panegyrics of remarkable merit. Using his inimitable resourcefulness with words and literary devices, he manoeuvered the ways of expression and mixed the simple with the complex to evolve a poetic language and style that then became his signature. His compositions speak softly to us; they are expostulations, at one time, and music and dialogues with the self about objective realities, at the other. His poetry is the embodiment of grace and dignity in times of decadence; it is marked by the imaginative awareness of cosmic reality and clear denial of orthodoxy. His complete Urdu poetry consists of six divaans, apart from his other works that include a biographical dictionary of Urdu poets, *Nukaatus Shu'araa*, a collection of five stories about sufis, *Faiz-e Mir*, an autobiography, *Zikr-e Mir*, and a collection of poems in Persian, *Kulliyaat-e Farsi*. Mir has been a model for succeeding generations of poets, and has been widely acknowledged by critics as an *ustad*, or master figure, in Urdu poetry. Many of them consider him a greater poet than Ghalib.

I

Raftagaan mein jahaan ke hum bhi hain
Saath us karwaan ke hum bhi hain

Shamma hi sar na de gaee barbaad
Kushta apni zabaan ke hum bhi hain

Hum ko Majnoon ko ishq mein mat poochh
Nang us khandaan ke hum bhi hain

Jis chamanzaar ka hai tu gul-e tar
Bulbul us gulsitaan ke hum bhi hain

Naheen Majoon se dil qawi lekin
Yaar us natawaan ke hum bhi hain

Bosa mat de kiso ke dar pe naseem
Khaak is aastaan ke hum bhi hain

Mar gaye mar gaye naheen to naheen
Khaak se munh ko dhaanke hum bhi hain

Apna shewa naheen kajee yoon to
Yaar ji tedhe baanke hum bhi hain

Wajh-e begaanagi naheen maloom
Tum jahaan ke ho waan ke hum bhi hain

Us sire ki hai parsaayi Mir
Motaqid us jawaan ke hum bhi hain

I

Of those who left the world behind, I too am one
Of that very passing caravan, I too am one

Not only has the burning lamp burnt my being
Scalded by my own tongue, I too am one

Don't ask how me and Majnoon lived in love
A sheer disgrace to that tribe, I too am one

Of the cherished garden, you are a proud blossom
A bulbul of that very garden, I too am one

Majnoon does not embolden me although
A friend of that feeble being, I too am one

Don't kiss anyone's door, take care, gentle breeze!
The soil of this threshold, I too am one

If I die, I die; if I don't, I don't
A face covered with soil, I too am one

It's not in me to act crooked, although
A turned and twisted one, I too am one

I do not know the cause for this indifference
That very place you come from, I too am one

My piety touches the highest peaks, Mir
But fervent for that youth, I too am one

2

Yaaro mujhe muaaf rakho main nashe mein hoon
Ab do to jaam khaali hi do main nashe mein hoon

Ek ek qart daur mein yoon hi mujhe bhi do
Jaam-e sharab pur na karo main nashe main hoon

Masti se darhami hai meri guftugu ke beech
Jo chaaho tum bhi mujh se kaho main nashe mein hoon

Ya haathon haath lo mujhe maanind-e jaam-e mai
Ya thodi door saath chalo main nashe mein hoon

Maazoor hoon jo paaon mera betarah pade
Tum sargaraan to mujh se na ho main nashe mein hoon

Bhaagi namaaz-e jum'a to jaati naheen hai kuchh
Chalta hoon main bhi tuk to raho main nashe main hoon

Nazuk mezaaj aap qayaamat hain Mir-ji
Joon sheesha mere munh na lago main nashe mein hoon

2

Forgive me, forgive me my friends, I'm so very drunk
If you must, give an empty cup, I'm so very drunk

In each round, please pour only a drop in my cup
Don't fill it please to the brim, I'm so very drunk

I'm so very drunk, I can't talk sense, I've gone berserk
Say what you wish, I can't care less, I'm so very drunk

Hold me my friend, just as you hold a cup of wine
Or just be in step with me, I'm so very drunk

I can't help it; I trip if I take a step
Don't be so upset with me, I'm so very drunk

The time for Juma prayers is not flying out yet
I too will come, just wait a bit, I'm so very drunk

Too delicate, Mir-ji, you are too fragile indeed
Don't tease me, as the wine glass does, I'm so very drunk

ROMANCE OF REALISM

The golden period of Urdu poetry that began with Mirza Mohammad Rafi Sauda and Mir Taqi Mir in the eighteenth century continued through the late eighteenth and mid-nineteenth centuries with a greater number of poets joining in to develop a larger and greater tradition of poetic excellence. There was a tendency in the poets to discover the elements of romance as also of realism, and to blend them together to mark the complex phenomenon of life and times. This period also saw the emergence of two *dabistaan* or literary schools—Lucknow and Delhi—and their distinct literary cultures that configured life and art in two distinct ways. The two schools also mark the two major aspects of the literary and social histories of Muslims. While the Lucknow school of poetry was represented by Sheikh Ghulam Ali Hamadani Mus'hafi, Syed Inshaallah Khan Insha, Qalandar Bakhsh Jur'at, Sheikh Imam Bakhsh Nasikh, and Khwaja Haider Ali Atish, the Delhi school was represented by

Bahadur Shah Zafar, Asadullah Khan Ghalib, Momin Khan
Momin, Nawab Mirza Khan Dagh Dehlavi, apart from Sheikh
Ibrahim Zauq and Mohammad Mustafa Khan Shefta. The
Lucknow poets treated language as an exquisite material and
played upon its splendour to versify delicate human passions.
In their bid to sound novel and appear distinct from the Delhi
school, they resorted to exaggeration, drew far-fetched images,
and discovered new turns of phrases by depending heavily on
Persian. This new literary culture also found a space in the
public imagination with the rising popularity of mushairas and
the emergence of poets as social icons, having their association
with the courts and nawabs. Even while poetry progressed in
Lucknow underscoring the experiences of life in a new language
of delicacy, it also showed a certain decline of literary taste in
some of the poets. This was reflected in their subservience to
their masters and their adherence to a stereotypical perception
of what could be treated as poetic and non-poetic in life and
literature. As opposed to these strains, the Delhi school poets
showed remarkable imaginative vitality, evolved a direct idiom,
spoke naturally, and carved space in their poetry for a larger
variety of experiences. Their poetry addressed issues that were
plebeian and patrician on the one hand, and philosophical and
spiritual on the other. They spoke in a secular language shining
bright with rare wit and humour. Delhi that had been ravaged
and rehabilitated again and again, both in the past and in the
present, with the first war of independence (1857) and the first
Delhi Durbar (1877), was lamented over and celebrated by its
poets now, as it was done before.

8

Sheikh Ghulam Ali Hamadani Mus'hafi

Sheikh Ghulam Ali Hamdani Mus'hafi (1750–1824), who was born in Ballamgarh near Delhi, spent his early life in Amroha, before moving to Delhi and finally settling down in Lucknow, where he lived until his death. He could not gain access to the Mughal court like several other poets who aspired for the same. As he was not well off, he even sold his verses for a living. It is said that Mus'hafi's divaan was stolen in Delhi, which added to his misery. This misery was doubled further with the constant literary rivalry he had with his contemporary, Inshaallah Khan Insha.

Mus'hafi was spontaneous in his rendition of verses which made him a prolific poet. Even though a substantial part of his poetic output deserves little attention, he also wrote verses that deserve serious critical attention. He approached his material with remarkable linguistic ease and combined the best traditions of the Delhi and Lucknow schools of poetry. This helped him take the Urdu language to new heights. Mus'hafi is marked for blending sensuality with mysticism, and taking his readers from the internal to the external world. His poetry is characterized by his keen sense of diction, his lyric grace, and his ability to apprehend the expected emotional response from the readers. Mus'hafi foreshadowed the modernist writers in that he broadened the frontiers of writing by connecting it to the writer's economic sustenance, rather than reiterating that a writer writes merely for the sake of writing and personal satisfaction. Mus'hafi has left behind two *tazkiraas* of Urdu poets, one of Persian poets, three divaans in Persian, eight in Urdu, and a book called *Majma-ul Fawaayid* about his life, love and sexuality.

I

Hai maah ke aftaab kya hai
Dekho to tah-e niqaab kya hai

Main ne tujhe tu ne mujh ko dekha
Ab mujh se tujhe hijaab kya hai

Aai ho to koee dam to baithho
Ai qibla ye izteraab kya hai

Us bin hamein jaagte hi guzri
Janaa na yehi ke khwaab kya hai

Mujhko bhi gine wo aashiqon mein
Is baat ka so hisaab kya hai

Seepara-i dil ko dekh us ne
poochha bhi na ye kitaab kya hai

Is maikada-i jahaan mein yaaro
Mujh saa bhi koee kharaab kya hai

Qismat mein hamaare Mus'hafi haai
Kya jaane sawaab azaab kya hai

I

The moon or the sun, what is there indeed?
Under the veil, look what is there indeed?

I have seen you, my love, you too have seen me
Then why a veil, in between, to share indeed?

If you have come, sit a while, don't hurry up
What's this impatience, what's that care indeed?

I've been awake in parting, ever awake
I don't know what a dream is, I swear indeed

She may count me too for her lover now—
How do I know, if she does care indeed?

She looked at the testament of heart but didn't ask
What book was that, what tome was there indeed?

In the tavern of this world, my dear friends
Is there one as bad as me, anyone there indeed?

My destiny Mus'hafi—Alas! Alas!
I do not know what sin is, what prayer is indeed!

2

Khwaab tha ya khayaal tha kya tha
Hijr tha ya wisaal tha kya tha

Chamki bijlee see per na samjhe hum
Husn tha ya jamaal tha kya tha

Mere pehlu main raat jaa kar wo
Maah tha ya hilaal tha kya tha

Shab jo do do haath uchhalta tha
Wajd tha ya wo haal tha kya tha

Jisko hum roz-e hijr samjhe the
Maah tha wo ke saal tha kya tha

Mus'hafi kal jo chup saa baithha tha
Kya tujhe kuchh malaal tha kya tha

2

A dream or a thought? What was that?
Parting or meeting? What was that?

Was that lightning? I could not guess
Beauty or splendour? What was that?

What lay by my side last night?
A moon, a crescent, what was that?

Last night he jumped in leaps and bounds
Rapture, frenzy, what was that?

What I thought was a separation
But a month or year? What was that?

Mus'hafi! What made you sit silent?
Some worry? Some care? What was that?

9

Syed Inshaallah Khan Insha

Syed Inshaallah Khan Insha (1757–1817) was born in Murshidabad, where his father, a royal physician, had shifted from Delhi when the city was passing through a period of chaos. Insha came to Delhi, and being a man of wit and novelty, got admittance in the court of Shah Alam II. Despairing at the failing powers of the Mughal court, he left for Lucknow, where he gained employment with Nawab Saadat Ali Khan as a poet-companion. Later, he resented the growing demands of the nawab who wanted him to write more and more verses while remaining in constant attendance. Relinquishing his job with the nawab, he spent the rest of his life in misery, penury and silence. His bitterness was further deepened with the ongoing literary brawls he had with his contemporary, Sheikh Ghulam Ali Hamadani Mus'hafi.

Insha was a sound scholar, a talented poet, an innovative prose writer and an extraordinary polyglot, who had a command over Arabic, Persian, Braj, Turkish, Pushto, Kashmiri, Punjabi, Marwari and Rekhti. This helped him towards developing an idiom for the ghazal, which had been growing and maturing continuously at the hands of other poets. He evolved the image of a protagonist in his ghazals, who represented the spirit of Lucknow as a centre of literature and culture. Interestingly, he also brought the Hindi idiom to bear upon his Urdu, which added yet another dimension to his urge for innovating language and broadening its frontiers. Insha has left behind a diverse literary capital that comprise his divaan, a major exemplar of literary, cultural and linguistic nuances in poetry, as well as prose works like *Silk-e Gohar*, a work of elegant Urdu fictional prose, *Raani Ketaki ki Kahaani*, a tale told without dependence on the Persian idiom, and *Daryaa-i Lataafat*, a discourse on language and rhetoric.

I

Kamar baandhe hue chalne ko yaan sab yaar baithhe hain
Bahut aage gaye baaqi jo hain taiyyaar baithhe hain

Na chhed ai nikhat-e baad-e bahaari raah lag apni
Tujhe atkheliyaan soojhi hain hum bezaar baithhe hain

Khayaal un ka pare hai arsh-e aazam se kaheen Saqi
Gharaz kuchh aur dhun mein is ghadi maikhwaar baithhe hain

Basaane naqsh-e paa-e rahrawaan kue tamanna mein
Naheen uthhne ki taaqat kya karein laachaar baithhe hain

Kahain hain sabr kis ko aah nang-o naam hai kya shai
Gharaz ro peet kar in sab ko hum ek baar baithhe hain

Najeebon ka ajab kuchh haal hai is daur mein yaaro
Jise poochho yehi kehta hai hum bekaar baithhe hain

Naee ye waz'a sharmaane ki sheekhi aaj hai tum ne
Hamaare paas saahab warna yoon sau baar baithhe hain

Kahaan gardish falak ki chayn deti hai hamein Insha
Ghaneemat hai ke hum soorat yahaan do chaar baithhe hain

I

Set to leave, all the fellows here are set to leave
Many have gone ahead, the rest are set to leave

Don't tease me, the fragrant breeze of spring! Don't!
You are toying with me; I'm tired now, set to leave

Their thoughts soar beyond the empyrean heights, Saqi
Sure of their own thoughts, the drunken ones are set to leave

They wish to leave their footprints in the lanes of desire
But the travellers lack the strength; they are set to leave

What is patience, or name, or fame, or shame, my friend!
We have lamented them all; we are now set to leave

The noble ones live a strange life now, my friends
They say it's all futile, so we are now set to leave

What's this coyness you have learnt of late, my love?
You loved my company then, but now I'm set to leave

The skies don't spare me a moment to think, Insha
Now, it's enough for us to sit apart and set to leave

2

Achha to khafaa hum se ho tum ai sanam achha
Lo hum bhi na bolenge Khuda ki qasam achha

Mashghool kiya chaahiye is dil ko kisee taur
Le levenge dhoond aur koee yaar hum achha

Garmi ne kuchh aag aur hi seene mein lagaa dee
Har taur gharaz aap se milna hai kam achha

Aghyaar se karte ho mere saamne baatein
Mujh per ye lage karne naya tum sitam achha

Hum motakif-e khilwat-e but khaana hain ai sheikh
Jaataa hai jaa tu pa-i su-e haram achha

Jo shakhsh muqeem-e rah-e dildaar hain zaahid
Firdaus lage un ko na baagh-e iram achha

Keh kar gaye aataa hoon koee dam mein main tum paas
Phir de chale kal ki see tarha mujh ko dum achha

Is hasti-i mauhoom se main tung hoon Insha
Wallah ke ab is se ba maraatib adam achha

2

Okay, you are angry with me my love, okay
I swear I too wouldn't speak to you, it's okay

I've to keep my heart busy, this or that way
I too will find myself a friend, it's okay

There is a heat in my breast; the breast burns in heat now
It's fine, I will meet you less and less, it's okay

You talk to others, while I look on helplessly
Okay, this is how you treat me now, it's okay

I'm retired to the idol house's seclusion, Sheikh
If you are going to the harem, go, it's okay

Those at the love's door and domain, dear devotee
Don't like heavens, or its gardens, it's okay

You leave saying you will be back in a while now
So, you plan to do what you did then, it's okay

I'm dead weary of this imagined life, Insha
Sure, the Eden is better by degrees, it's okay

10

Bahadur Shah Zafar

Bahadur Shah Zafar (1775–1862) is the nom de plume of
Mirza Abu Zafar Sirajuddin Mohammad Bahadur Shah Zafar.
History remembers this last Mughal emperor as Bahadur Shah
II and literature as Bahadur Shah Zafar. After the first battle
of Independence in 1857, he was arrested, his three sons killed
and their heads hung on the gate in Delhi, now known as Delhi
Gate. He was later tried in Calcutta and exiled in Rangoon, now
Yangon in Myanmar, where he died and was buried with no
trace of his grave for a long time, as he had predicted. There
stands a shrine now at the supposed site.

A poet, a kind patron of poets, an aesthete and a man of
religious leaning, Zafar was a disciple of Shah Naseer, Sheikh
Ibrahim Zauq and Mirza Ghalib. For him, composing poetry
was cultivating a difficult art that called for perseverance and
devotion. This also explains his choice for multi-syllabic lines
and difficult *qaafia* and *radeef*. He is also remarkable for the

local colour he added to his poetry and his sensitivity towards the music that helped him modulate his tone of voice. Zafar wrote the characteristic poetry of love and despair in his early writing phase and of more serious concerns like the failings of the human destiny during his exile. Though some Urdu critics did not view his poetry favourably, but he also emerged as a sensitive commentator on the fall of the Mughal Empire. Zafar had compiled four divaans before 1857 though much was lost during the turbulent events of that year.

I

Baat karni mujhe mushkil kabhi aisi to na thi
Ab hai jaisi teri mehfil kabhi aisi to na thi

Le gaya chheen ke yoon kaun tera sabr-o-qaraar
Beqaraari tujhe ai dil kabhi aisi to na thi

Un ki aankhon ne Khuda jaane kiya kya jaadoo
Ke tabeeyat meri maayil kabhi aisi to na thi

Ab ke jo raah-e mohabbat mein uthhaai takleef
Sakht hoti hamein manzil kabhi aisi to na thi

Paai khubaan koee zindaan mein naya hai majnoon
Aaee aawaaz-e salaasil kabhi aisi to na thi

Chashm-e qaatil meri dushman thi hamesha lekin
Jaisi ab ho gaee qaatil kabhi aisi to na thi

Aks-e rukhsaar ne kis ke hai tujhe chamkaaya
Taab tujh mein mah-e kaamil kabhi aisi to na thi

Nigah-i yaar ko ab kyun hai taghaaful ai dil
Wo tere haal se ghaafil kabhi aisi to na thi

Kya sabab tu jo bigadtaa hai Zafar pe har baar
Khoo teri hoor shamaayil kabhi aisi to na thi

I

It was never so very hard to speak, but now
Your assembly was never so bleak, but now

Who robbed you of your patience, my poor heart?
Never so restless and ever so meek, but now

What magic in her glance, I never knew!
I would so much crave for and seek, but now

So hard this time to bear the pangs of love
My goal was never so oblique, but now

There in the prison house, a wild lover
Whose chains did never so shriek, but now

Love's glances torment me, as they always do
Never these torments at such a peak, but now

Whose glowing face brightens your face, O moon!
Your glow was never so unique, but now

Why doesn't my love look at me, my heart!
My love was never so bleak, but now

But why such anger with Zafar each time
Such revenge, you would never wreak, but now

2

Hum to chalte hain lo Khuda Haafiz
Butkadaa ke buto Khuda Haafiz

Kar chuke tum naseehatein hum ko
Jaao bus naaseho Khuda Haafiz

Aaj kuchh aur tarha per un ki
Sunte hain guftugoo Khuda Haafiz

Gar yahi hai hamesha zakhm pe zakhm
Dil ke chaara garo Khuda Haafiz

Aaj hai kuchh ziyaada betaabi
Dil-e betaab ko Khuda Haafiz

Kyun hifaazat hum aur ki dhoondein
Har nafas jab ke ho Khuda Haafiz

Chaahe rukhsat ho raah-e ishq mein 'aql
Ai Zafar jaane do Khuda Haafiz

2

Goodbye friends, I'm set to go, Khuda Haafiz
All my idols in a row, Khuda Hafiz

Enough of counsels! My dear counsellors!
Just leave me now, let me go, Khuda Haafiz

In a different tone and tenor, my friends
I can now hear his words flow, Khuda Haafiz

Wound after wound, one by one, dear healers
You've kept my heart all aglow, Khuda Haafiz

Today, my impatience far exceeds my pain
It keeps my poor heart on toe, Khuda Haafiz

What protection from anyone now, my friend
When to me, my own breaths blow, Khuda Haafiz

If reason can be so lost to love, Zafar
Why care then, let it be so, Khuda Haafiz

II

Sheikh Imam Bakhsh Nasikh

Sheikh Imam Bakhsh Nasikh (1776–1838) was born in Faizabad and later travelled to Lucknow. He had his education in Arabic and Persian. On account of his keen poetic sensibility and sound training in rhetoric, he had his disciples among the nobility. A man of integrity, he did not, however, vie for reaping any benefits from them. In fact, he became a victim of serious political bickering and left Lucknow for Allahabad.

Nasikh earned his reputation not as a great poet but as a great craftsman of poetry. He deliberated upon language, syntax and the poetic devices, which he employed to turn a routine composition into a work of art. Literary circles in Delhi came to hear of his worth, and considered him worth emulating. He played a significant role in secularizing Urdu while respecting the classical norms of syntax and style. In doing this, he expanded the frontiers of Urdu vocabulary, adopted a non-puritanical approach, and modernized it. His individuality lies in imparting an Indo-Persian veneer to his verse. This also explains his kinship with poets like Mirza Mohammad Rafi Sauda, Mir Taqi Mir and Khwaja Mir Dard, who also deliberated upon the nature and function of language and the modes of poetic expression. Not a poet of great metaphysical depth, Nasikh's merit lies in his technical virtuosity, linguistic finesse and his ability to control and modulate intricate lines and unusual rhythms. These qualities are well borne out by his several divaans.

I

Sanam koocha tera hai aur main hoon
Ye zindaan-e daghaa hai aur main hoon

Yehi kehtaa hai jalwa mere but kaa
Ke ik zaat-e Khuda hai aur main hoon

Idhar aane mein hai kis se tujhe sharm
Faqat ik gham tera hai aur main hoon

Kare jo har qadam per ek naala
Zamaane mein daraa hai aur main hoon

Teri deewaar se aati hai aawaaz
Ke ek baal-e huma hai aur main hoon

Na ho kuchh aarzoo mujh ko khudaaya
Yehi har dam dua hai aur main hoon

Kiya darbaan ne sang-e aastaana
Dar-e daulat saraa hai aur main hoon

Gaya wo chhod kar raste mein mujh ko
Ab us ka naqsh-e paa hai aur main hoon

Zamaane ke sitam se roz Nasikh
Naee ek Karbala hai aur main hoon

I

My love, this is your lane and this is me
This prison house of deceit and this is me

This is what my love's splendour tells me now:
There is the God above; here this is me

What makes you shy of coming to me, Love?
This is love's pain with me and this is me

It moans at each step in life, as it does
That is the time's bell tolling and this is me

From your walls, there often comes a clear call
There's the phoenix hair there and here this is me

Let me never nurse a desire, my God, never
That is my perpetual prayer and this is me

The guard of love's abode turned me to a doorstep
This is my own love's threshold and this is me

She left me alone on the way forever
These are her footprints for me and this is me

The world has been unkind each day, Nasikh
This is a new Karbala and this is me

2

Aati jaati hai jaa ba jaa badli
Saaqiya jald aa hawaa badli

Aage the gard ab hai boo-i saman
Too ne poshak ai sabaa badli

Barg-e tar aai barg-e khushk gire
Har shajar ne bhi ab qabaa badli

Rang chehre ke yaan badalne lage
Aankh teri jahaan zaraa badli

Rind maikhwaar jab pukarte hain
Door se deti hai sadaa badli

2

Here and there blow the clouds with the change of wind
My dear Saqi, come on fast, it's the change of wind

You were dust then; you are blossom's fragrance now
Wind! You have changed your garb with the change of wind

New leaves may show up now, while old ones may fall
May the bough change her garb with the change of wind

All the well-known faces changed with the change of time
Only when your eyes turned with the change of wind

Only when the drunken vagabonds give a shout
The clouds echo from afar with the change of wind

12

Khwaja Haider Ali Atish

Khwaja Haider Ali Atish (1777–1847), who hailed from a Sufi family of Delhi, was born in Faizabad and travelled to nearby Lucknow, the goal of all literary dilettantes and masters. Neither associated with a *durbaar* or the court of the nobles, nor influenced by the privileged and the powerful, Atish enjoyed his self-respect and courage of conviction. True to his spirit, he refused to be carried away by the splendour of people in high places, and preferred to lead the life of a liberal Sufi and devote himself to the vocation of poetry.

Atish was a disciple of Sheikh Ghulam Ali Hamadani Mus'hafi. Striking a balance between the odds and the evens, he was now spontaneous, now remote; now restrained, now sentimental; now ratiocinative, now mystical. He was extremely resourceful with the Urdu idiom and played upon the softness of its tone. His sincere sentiments and robust command over language blended well to create a condition of lasting appeal.

Even while he maintained a uniform level of expression, he turned wordy and flamboyant at times, but remained simple and eminently accessible. Atish chose to philosophize on the pleasures of flesh and delve deeper to express the ecstatic moments of union. In his essential literary make-up, he drew upon his healthy attitude towards life and art to bring life to bear upon art, and art on life. Atish has left behind two divaans that exemplify his independent and proud poetic stance.

I

Sun to sahi jahaan mein hai tera fasaana kyaa
Kehti hai tujh se khalq-e Khuda ghaibaana kyaa

Zair-e zameen aata hai jo gul so zarbakaf
Qaroon ne raaste mein lutaaya khazana kyaa

Udtaa hai shauq-e raahat-e manzil se asp-e 'umr
Mahmaiz kahte hainge kise taazyaana kyaa

Zeena saba ka dhoondti hai apni musht-e khaak
Baam-e baland yaar ka hai aastaana kyaa

Chaaron taraf se soorat-e jaanan ho jalwagar
Dil saaf ho tera to hai aaeena khaana kyaa

Tabl-o alam hi paas hai apne na mulk-o-maal
Hum se khilaaf ho ke karega zamaana kyaa

Aati hai kis tarah se meri qabz-e rooh ko
Dekhoon to maut dhoond rahi hai bahaana kyaa

Hota hai zard sun ke jo naraaz muddaee
Rustam ki daastaan hai hamaaraa fasaana kyaa

Tirchhi nazar se taair-e dil ho chuka shikaar
Jab teer kaj pade to udegaa nishaana kyaa

Yoon muddaee hasad se na de daad to na de
Atish ghazal ye too ne kahi aashiqaana kyaa

I

Just see what tale the world has this day for me
Just hear what this creation has to say for me

Such rich blossoms within the soil! They are in hand
What treasures Qaroon frittered, that's no array for me

Life's stallion flies high to kiss the joys of arrival
What's a spur! What's a whip! What's there to say for me

My body's soil wants to climb the stairs of wind
To reach my love's station that's so far away for me

Let there be nothing around, only my love's face
My heart mirrors me, what is the mirror's array for me?

I have no armours, no flags; I have none to flaunt
What can the world do if it goes astray for me?

Let me see if she may rob me of my life now
Let me also see if death can find a way for me

The complainant goes pale, dry, dull and desolate
Is Rustum's story but only a replay for me?

A twisted look has hit the heart's delicate bird
With awry arrow amiss, nothing to say for me

Who cares if the rivals don't say a word of praise
What a ghazal of love Atish wrote today for me

2

Tasawwur se kisee ke main ne kee hai guftugoo barson
Rahi hai ek tasweer-e khayaali ru-baroo barson

Hua mehmaan aa kar raat bhar wo shama ru barson
Rahaa raushan mere ghar ka chiraagh-e aarzoo barson

Chaman mein jaa ke bhoole se main khasta dil karaahaa tha
Kiya ki gul se bulbul shikwa-i dard-e guloo barson

Baraabar jaan ke rakkha hai us ko marte marte tak
Hamaari qabr per roya karegi aarzoo barson

Diya hai hukm jab peer-e mughan ne sajda-i khum ka
Kiya hai jab sharaab-e naab se hum ne wuzoo barson

Agar main khaak bhi hoonga to Atish gard-e baad aasa
Rakhegi mujh ko sargashta kisee ki justujoo barson

2

I have chatted with her fine thoughts for years
An imagined one I have sought for, for years

She lived many a night with me for years
I kept my yearning so well-wrought for years

In despair, I moaned only once in the garden
To the buds, the bulbul moaned her lot for years

I have to keep my longing close to heart till I die
To shed them on my grave, tears are sought for years

I could bow down to the wine jar, the priest ruled, only if
Pure wine ablution, I did and sought for years

If I be dust, I shall be one with the wind, Atish
A quest for someone will keep me distraught for years

13

Asadullah Khan Ghalib

Asadullah Khan Ghalib (1797–1869), hailing from the central Asian family of Aibuk Turks, was born in Agra. His grandfather had migrated to India during the reign of Shah Alam II and joined the army, which his sons also did after him. After his father was killed in a battle in Alwar, Ghalib had to live a life of want and longing. Inheriting little from his family, he made plea after plea with the British government for his own pension for over sixteen years but only to little avail. Grants in appreciation from the last Mughal emperor and the Nawab of Rampur kept him going somehow. He witnessed the downfall of the Mughal Empire and the Revolt of 1857, which he frankly recorded in his poetry and prose. He earned three coveted titles from Bahadur Shah Zafar II, although he was not very well appreciated during his lifetime.

Ghalib's literary identities are many. He was an accomplished poet and a prose writer, an epistolarian and a diarist, a lexicographer and a polemist, a critic and a historian, and above all, an arbiter of taste. He had compiled his Urdu divaan by the age of twenty-five. By this time, he had also developed a keen interest in Persian writing, of which his Persian divaan is a rich testimony. He enriched the literary traditions of Urdu and Persian with his unique improvisations in form and technique. Ghalib's wit remains unparalleled and his diction refreshingly original. While Ghalib recorded his pain in his inimitable letters in no uncertain terms, his diary called *Dustumboo*, detailing the events of 1857, is a cautious and political act of writing. Other works include his Urdu divaan, *Mehr-e Neem Roze*, a historical narrative; *Panj Aahang*, a collection of miscellaneous writings; *Qat-i Burhaan*, a criticism of Persian lexicon; and *Tegh-i Tez*, a work of literary criticism. Ghalib remains, till this day, the most contemporaneous of all the literary masters in Urdu and in Persian.

I

Dil-e naadaan tujhe hua kya hai
Aakhir is dard ki dawaa kya hai

Hum hain mushtaaq aur wo bezaar
Ya Ilahi ye maajraa kya hai

Main bhi munh mein zabaan rakhtaa hoon
Kaash poochho ke mudd'aa kya hai

Jab ke tujh bin nahi koee maujood
Phir ye hungaama ay Khuda kya hai

Ye pari chehra log kaise hain
Ushwa-o ghamza-o adaa kya hai

Shikan-e zulf-e ambarein kyun hai
Nigah-e chashm-e surma saa kya hai

Sabza-o gul kahaan se aai hain
Abr kya cheez hai hawaa kya hai

Hum ko un se wafaa ki hai ummeed
Jo naheen jaanate wafaa kya hai

I

My naive heart, what ails you, what?
What's the cure for this ache, what?

I pine for her; she's tired of me
My God! What's the matter, what?

I too have a tongue in my mouth
Wish you asked: what matters, what?

There is none around but you
What then is this hubbub, what?

Who are these fairy-faced, who?
What dainty, mild manners, what?

Such curls in scented locks, why?
What glance, collyrium-eyes, what?

Where from the meadows, blossoms?
What is that cloud, this wind, what?

I want love, loyalty from one
For whom love and loyalty, what?

Haan bhalaa kar tera bhalaa hoga
Aur darwesh ki sadaa kya hai

Jaan tum per nisaar kartaa hoon
Main naheen jaantaa du'aa kya hai

Main ne maanaa ke kuchh naheen Ghalib
Muft haath aai to buraa kya hai

'Do good, get good from others'
What else is dervish-chant, what?

I simply lay this life for you
I know not what prayer, what?

I know, Ghalib is no good
What if he comes for free, what?

2

Aah ko chaahiye ik umr asar hote tak
Kaun jeeta hai teri zulf ke sar hote tak

Daam-e har mauj mein hai halqa-i sad kaam-e nahang
Dekhein kya guzre hai qatre pe gohar hote tak

Aashiqi sabr talab aur tamannaa betaab
Dil ka kya rang karoon khoon-e jigar hote tak

Hum ne maana ke taghaaful na karoge lekin
Khaak ho jaaenge hum tum ko khabar hote tak

Partaw-e khur se hai shabnam ko fanaa ki taaleem
Main bhi hoon ek inaayat ki nazar hote tak

Ek nazar besh nahi fursat-e hasti ghaafil
Garmiy-i bazm hai ik raqs-e sharar hote tak

Gham-e hasti ka Asad kis se ho juz marg ilaaj
Shama har rung mein jalti hai sehar hote tak

2

My wails need a lifetime to reach the heart, wait, O wait
But who can live that long to see it reach, wait, O wait

Hundred circles in each eddy, hundred crocodiles too
See what happens till the drops become pearls, wait, O wait

Love demands patience; desire takes no pleas ever
What to do till my heart breathes her last, wait, O wait

I'm sure you would not be careless; would surely pay heed
But I would be ashes before you said, wait, O wait

The dew has learnt of dying only from the sunrays
I too will live till I get a kind look, wait, O wait

O the careless one! Life would not give you a wink more
The assembly is agog till flames dance, wait, O wait

But who can cure the pains of life and living, Asad?
The lamp burns in every hue till dawn's break, wait, O wait

14

Momin Khan Momin

Momin Khan Momin (1800–1851), whose father and grandfather were court physicians, was born, educated and settled in Delhi. He received his education at the famous Shah Abdul Qadir's school, under the coveted guidance of Shah Abdul Aziz, a celebrated theologian and reformer of the times. Momin received a wide exposure to a variety of disciplines including medicine, mathematics and astrology as well as to languages like Arabic, Persian and Urdu. Music and chess were his other areas of keen interest which he cultivated with care.

Momin was essentially a poet of romantic love which he expressed best in the form of ghazal. The lover in his poetry is one of amorous disposition; he expresses his love along with lust, and sees lust as a part of life's romance. As Momin dwelt upon the psychology of the lover, he explored his moods and reflexes, as also his erotic and sexual tendencies. In celebrating romantic love in all its manifestations, he drew upon the chastity of diction, mixing deeply nuanced phrases for a metaphysical apprehension of the phenomenon of love and the figure of the lover. Momin was an aesthete; he personalized his material which distinguishes him from many other poets who objectified them. Apart from his Urdu divaan, Momin also left behind a Persian divaan, and other works in prose.

I

Asar us ko zaraa naheen hota
Ranj raahat fizaa naheen hota

Bewafaa kahne ki shikaayat hai
To bhi waada wafaa naheen hota

Kis ko hai zauq talkh kaami ka
Jung bin kuchh mazaa naheen hota

Tum hamaare kisee tarah na hue
Warna dunya mein kyaa naheen hota

Imtehaan keejiye mera jab tak
Shauq zor aazmaa naheen hota

Naarsaayi se dum ruke to ruke
Main kisee se khafaa naheen hota

Tum mere pass hote ho goya
Jab koee doosaraa naheen hota

Haal-e dil yaar ko likhoon kyunkar
Haath dil se judaa naheen hota

Daaman us ka jo hai daraaz to ho
Dast-e aashiq rasaa naheen hota

Chara-i-dil sewaai sabr naheen
So tumhaare siwa naheen hota

Kyun sune arz-e muztarab Momin
Sanam aakhir Khuda naheen hota

I

She takes no pretence, no pleas
Misery brings no calm, no ease

She resents being called faithless
But meets her promise so less

Whoever likes to speak bitter
But no pleasure without jitters

You couldn't be mine for all I did
Or else, the world would be my bid

You test me as long as you wish
But my wishes can't be selfish

The breath may lose track in despair
But my displeasure would be rare

You are mine when none else is mine
None else but you alone are mine

How to write, my love, how's my heart
I can't take my hand off my heart

Sure, that kindness may be endless
Sure, but lovers don't seek access

Patience alone may save the heart
Heart has no patience with you apart

Why should Momin implore for a nod
She is only my love, not my God

2

Royaa karenge aap bhi pehron isee tarah
Atka kaheen jo aap ka dil bhi meri tarah

Aataa naheen hai wo to kisee dhab se daao mein
Banti naheen hai milne ki us se koee tarah

Tashbeeh kis se doon ke tarah daar ki mere
Sab se niraali waza hai sab se naee tarah

Mar chuk kaheen ke tu gham-e hijraan se chhoot jaai
Kahte to hain bhale ki wa lekin buri tarah

Nay taab hijr mein hai na aaraam wasl mein
Kambakht dil ko chayn naheen hai kisee tarah

Lagti hain gaaliyan bhi tere munh se kya bhali
Qurbaan tere! Phir mujhe keh ley isee tarah

Paamaal hum na hote faqat jaur-e charkh se
Aai hamaari jaan pe aafat kaee tarah

Maashooq aur bhi hain bataa de jahaan mein
Kartaa hai kaun zulm kisee per teri tarah

Nay jaai waan bane hai na bin jaai chayn hai
Kya keejiye hamein to hai mushkil sabhee tarah

Hoon jaan balab butaan-e sitamgar ke haath se
Kya sab jahaan mein jeete hain Momin isee tarah

2

You would see no end ever, you too would cry like me
Ensnared in this love, you too would ever sigh like me

I can't take her in confidence, whatever I do
I can't even see her; I can only sigh like me

What similes can I bring for my stylish love
Can't describe her form and moving if I try like me

'Die a death; seek a release from the pains of parting'
That's only a truth but harshly told to die like me

There's no patience in parting, in meeting no relief
This very silly heart of mine can only vie like me

Even the abuses from your sweet lips sound so sweet
I would just bet my life, take me on and try like me

I wouldn't be ruined ever only by the divine will
But I had many a blow to help me die like me

There are so many lovers here but does anyone
Ever bear the pains of loving just to die like me

I'm restless if I go to her, restive if I don't
There is no letting go, I can only die like me

I count my breath, Momin, thanks to my unkind love
Do all the lovers in this world decry like me?

15

Nawab Mirza Khan Dagh Dehlavi

Nawab Mirza Khan Dagh Dehlavi (1831–1905) was born and brought up in the Red Fort of Delhi, where his mother was married to Prince Mirza Mohammad Sultan, son of Bahadur Shah Zafar II. After his father's death, he had to leave the Red Fort, and after the fall of Delhi in 1857, he had to move to Rampur where he lived in comfort for more than a decade. Later, his changing fortunes, for good or bad, took him to other centres of renown like Lucknow, Patna, Calcutta and Hyderabad.

As a disciple of Sheikh Ibrahim Zauq himself, and with many eminent disciples to his own credit, Dagh deliberated upon the aesthetic principles of ghazal as a form of intimate poetic conversation. He charged the common speech and combined the poetic manners of the Lucknow and Delhi schools. In its totality, Dagh's poetry is idiomatic and appealing, laden with emotions and good humour. He did not take the idea of love to philosophical heights but engaged with the experience of love at a human level, bringing it close to eroticism. Cumulatively, he is playful with language, least Persianized in his diction, witty with the turn of phrases, urbane in addressing, and full of gaiety and simplicity in the quintessential approach to his material. Apart from his four divaans, representing the last hallmarks of classical poetry, he has left behind a bunch of letters and a narrative poem on his love-life, titled *Faryaad-e Dagh*.

I

Uzr aane mein bhi hai aur bulaate bhi naheen
Baa'is-e tark-e mulaaqaat bataate bhi naheen

Muntazir hai dam-e rukhsat ke ye jaai to jaaein
Phir ye ehsaan ke hum chhod ke jaate bhi naheen

Sar uthhaao to sahi aankh milaao to sahee
Nasha-i mai bhi naheen neend ke maate bhi naheen

Kya kaha phir to kaho hum nahi sunte teri
Naheen sunte to hum aison ko bataate bhi naheen

Khoob pardaa hai ke chilman se lage baithhe hain
Saaf chhupte bhi naheen saamne aate bhi naheen

Mujh se laaghar teri aankhon mein khatakte to rahe
Tujh se naazuk meri aankhon mein samaate bhi naheen

Daikhte hi teri mehfil mein ye irshaad hua
Kaun baithha hai ise log uthhaate bhi naheen

Ho chuka tark-e ta'alluq to jafaaein kyun hon
Jin ko matlab nahi rehtaa wo sataate bhi naheen

Zeest se tang ho ai Dagh to jeete kyun ho
Jaan pyari bhi naheen jaan se jaate bhi naheen

I

She has a plea for not coming, doesn't call me either
But her reasons for not coming, doesn't tell me either

She waits for my last breath to say the last goodbye
Just to show her favour to me she can't leave either

Now lift your head, look into my eyes and let me see
Love! You are neither so drunk, nor so sleepy either

What did you say; say again, that you wouldn't listen to me
If you wouldn't, I too wouldn't say a word to you either

What a veil you keep, my love, hanging close to lattice
Being not so fully hidden, showing not so fully either

Such a frail one like me has irked your eyes forever
So a delicate one like you can't fit my eyes either

Just as she spotted me in the assembly, she said
Who's this sitting here, why isn't he removed either?

Now that we have parted, why should we ever pretend?
We being such strangers, we should not bother either

If so tired of this life, why do you live this life, Dagh?
It's not dear to you; you don't leave this life either

2

Dil gaya tum ne liya hum kya karein
Jaane waali cheez thee gham kya karein

Hum ne mar kar hijr mein paayi shafa
Aise achhon ka wo maatam kya karein

Apne hi gham se naheen milti nijaat
Is benaa per fikr-e 'aalam kya karein

Kar chuke sab apni apni hikmatein
Dum nikaltaa ho to hum dum kya karein

Poore honge apne armaan kis tarah
Shauq behad waqt hai kam kya karein

Bakhsh bhi dein pyar ki gustakhiyaan
Dil hi qaaboo mein naheen hum kya karein

Tund khoo hai kab sune wo dil ki baat
Aur bhi barham ko barham kya karein

Aik saaghar per hai apni zindagi
Rafta rafta is se bhi kam kya karein

Dil ne seekha shewa-i begaanagi
Aise naamehram ko mehram kya karein

2

You robbed me of my heart, what can I do?
It was meant to be robbed, what can I do?

I got my cure when I died in parting
If none to mourn such a one, what can I do?

I cannot get release from my own pains ever
How can I worry for the world, what can I do?

All of them have tried their hands to save that love
If she breathes last, what can you do, what can I do?

How can I fulfil my desires, how indeed?
Desires aplenty, time short, what can I do?

Forgive me my insolence in love, my love
If the heart gets out of hand, what can I do?

She is quick-tempered; she does not listen to me
Why annoy the annoyed one, what can I do?

My life rests now on a cup of wine for me
Now live on less than a cup? What can I do?

You know so well how to turn a stranger
To make the stranger a friend, what can I do?

Muamila hai aaj husn-o-ishq ka
Dekhiye wo kya karein hum kya karein

Aaeena hai aur wo hain dekhiye
Faisala donon ye baaham kya karein

Keh rahe ahl-e sifaarish mujh se Dagh
Teri qismat hai buri hum kya karein

It's a matter between a lover and the beloved
Now let me see what she does, what can I do?

This is a mirror and that is she, just see
They must decide by themselves, what can I do?

Those who hold a plea for me, tell me, Dagh
You surely have bad luck, what can I do?

ADVENT OF MODERNISM

It was during the mid-nineteenth century that the Urdu ghazal showed the first signs of what may be called the 'modern' sensibility. After the first war of independence (1857), life and times had greatly changed. The days of the nobles being patrons to the poets were over, as lives of luxury and glamour associated with Delhi and Lucknow had become stories of the past. The poet was now a common man left on his own, living in an age of great socio-political transition. He had to grapple with the realities of the new world and expand the frontiers of his knowledge and perception. He had to reconfigure his idiom and reorient his metaphor to execute his uniquely different experiences in a language liberated from the constraints of the iconic Persian. As there was no room left for the purely romantic perceptions of life and for linguistic mannerisms, the poets were to evolve a new poetics for their new age. Thus, they tried to discover their modes of discernment and expression by adhering partially to the older norms, now rejecting them altogether, but most often, by striking a balance between the two. They replaced the old myths of love and longing with the new metaphors of human bonding, just as they replaced the traditional penchant for sentimentality with irony and rationality. They expanded the hinterlands of traditional references to find space for the mundane and the metaphysical, along with the political and the apolitical. In doing this, they operated in a larger frame of references to present a world-view of greater complexity. These poets defined the tone and tenor of the modern ghazal broadly until the mid-twentieth century, but more importantly, they made way for the emergence of newer versions of the modernist ghazal in the more consequential decades of the twentieth century.

The lingering shadows of Macaulay's Minutes on Education (1835), Charles Wood's despatch on education (1854) and the first war of independence (1857) fell on the current realities, which included Gandhi's arrival on the Indian scene (1914), the Khilafat and Non-Cooperation movements (1920), the Civil Disobedience Movement (1930), the Government of India Act (1935), the Independence and Partition of India (1947) and the dawn of the new Indian state. These were directly or indirectly, metaphorically or mythically, represented by a larger variety of poets with diverse social, cultural, political and philosophical affiliations.

16

Khwaja Altaf Hussain Hali

Khwaja Altaf Hussain Hali (1837–1914) was born in Panipat, where he also received his early education. On coming to Delhi, he learnt Arabic and Persian and received patronage from two major poets, Mirza Asadullah Khan Ghalib and Mohammad Mustafa Khan Shefta. After Shefta's death, he left for Lahore and joined the Punjab Government Book Depot, where he got an opportunity to read Western literature. Hali paid serious heed to Mohammad Hussain Azad's call for the new Urdu poem and Sir Syed Ahmad Khan's call for rationalism in social, political and educational matters of the Muslims. These two influences determined his future course of development as a poet, critic, commentator, biographer and translator.

Hali started writing as a poet of the traditional Urdu ghazal. Later, he initiated a more serious phase of his literary career, which also marked the beginning of modernism in Urdu literature. He made a major case for simplicity of expression and seriousness of thought and purpose. His engagement with the writing of ameliorative poetry explains his distaste for the panegyric ghazal which, he argued, could no longer sustain the burden of new consciousness. Instead, he emphasized the contemporary relevance of narrative poetry and made a case for 'natural poetry', shorn of sentimentality and tied to reality. While Hali wrote in various forms, he developed a composite view of life and art in close association with each other. His *Muqaddama-i Sher-o shairi* is, in many respects, the first critical manifesto of Urdu poetry, like Wordsworth's 'Preface to the Lyrical Ballads'. It is an anthology of ideas concerning the nature of true art, its language, the parameters of its creation, and the making of taste. In *Madd-o jazar-e Islam*, he reflected upon the trials and travails of Islam. In *Tiryaaq-e Masmoom*, he developed a discourse on religious disputation, while in *Majaalis-un Nisaa*, he projected an argument in favour of women's' education in a fictional framework. *Tabaqaat-ul Arz* is his translation of an Arabic discourse. Hali wrote sober and scientific prose, plain and persuasive poetry, broadly representing a case of art for life's sake. Hali's biographies of Sir Syed Ahmad Khan, Asadullah Khan Ghalib and Persian poet Shekhi Sadi remain authentic sources till this day.

I

Hai justujoo ke khoob se hai khoob tar kahaan
Ab thhehrti hai dekhiye jaa kar nazar kahaan

Hain daur-e jaam awwal-e shab mein khudi se door
Hoti hai aaj dekhiye hum ko sahar kahaan

Yaa Rab is ikhtilaat ka anjaam ho bakhair
Thaa us ko hum se rubt magar is qadar kahaan

Ek 'umr chaahiye ke gawaara ho naish-e ishq
Rakhhi hai aaj lazzat-e zakhm-e jigar kahaan

Bus ho chuka bayaan kasal-o ranj raah ka
Khat ka mere jawaab hai ai nama bar kahaan

Koon-o makaan se hai dil-e wahshi kinaara geer
Is khanama kharaab ne dhoondä hai ghar kahaan

Hum jis pe mar rahe hain wo hai baat hi kuchh aur
Aalam mein tujh se laakh sahi too magar kahaan

Hoti nahin qubool dua tark-e ishq ki
Dil chahtaa na ho to dua mein asar kahaan

Hali nishaat-e naghma-o mai dhoondte ho ab
Aai ho waqt-e sub'h rahe raat bhar kahaan

130

I

My quest keeps me alert: where's the best—here or there?
Let's see where the chase comes to an end—here or there

The rounds of drink at early night aren't cared for much
See, where I see the morn, if I do, here or there

God! Let this intimacy reach a happy end
She knew me well, earlier as well—here or there

It needs a lifetime to endure the stings of love
Tell me where lie the pleasures of pain—here or there

Enough of telling the tales of journey's woe but
Where is the reply to my message, here or there?

The wild heart stays away from all the world
Where has this vagrant heart found a home, here or there?

What makes me sad is not this, surely something else
With millions around, there's none like you—here or there

The prayer to forsake love cannot be answered
With a heart unwilling, it would not reach—here or there

Hali! You look for pleasures of wine and music now
You came at the dawn, but whither all night—here or there?

2

Kuchh hansi khel sambhalnaa gham-e hijraan mein naheen
Chaak dil mein hai mere jo ke garebaan mein naheen

Kis tarha us ki lagaawat ko banaawat samjhoon
Khat mein likkhaa hai wo alqaab jo unwaan mein naheen

Dee hai waa'iz ne kin aadaab ki takleef na poochh
Aise uljhaao teri kaakul-e pechaan mein naheen

Beqaraari thee sub ummeed-e mulaqaat ke saath
Ab wo agli si daraazi shab-e hijraan mein naheen

Hali-i zaar ko kehte hain ke hai shaahid baaz
Ye to aasaar kuchh us mard-e musalmaan mein naheen

2

Bearing the pangs of parting is no joke, not the least
The heart is ripped apart, but the robes, not the least

Her care is real, no pretence, no, of course, not
Her manners tell me, not the contents, not the least

Don't ask how stringent the preacher's sermons are
But no such traps in your tresses, not the least

My eager heart's hope for our union keeps me alive
Now the night of parting is not that long, not the least

Poor Hali is blamed to be all the sweethearts' throb
But is that a faith-keeper's way? No, not the least

17

Shad Azimabadi

Shad Azimabadi (1846–1927) was born Syed Ali Mohammad in Azimabad, now Patna. He received traditional education rather early in his life and learnt Urdu, Persian and Arabic. This was followed by his own studies of Islam and other religions which turned him into a liberal humanist. Although Shad hailed from an affluent family, he cared less for riches, and even lesser for the sources of his future sustenance. Following the general practice of poets in the making, he too received counselling on his poetry from several master craftsmen. As he emerged as a poet of remarkable merit and a sound scholar, he earned the title of Khan Bahadur from the British government, with a monthly stipend of a thousand rupees.

Shad was essentially a poet of the ghazal tradition. He was no philosopher; nor did he have a taste for stereotypical themes. He distinguished himself because of his refreshing ideas and novel ways of expression. He engaged with issues in ethics, philosophy and mysticism, as he deliberated on the unity of God. Following Mir Babar Ali Anis, the celebrated poet of *marsiya*, or the elegy, he also practised this form. A full-time poet and writer, Shad has left behind a formidable oeuvre. Some of his most important works include a biography titled *Hayaat-e Faryaad*, a historical tract titled *Nawa-i Watan*, his collected poems in *Kulliyaat-e Shad* and *Maikhana-i Ilhaam*, and an account of *marsiya* poets, titled *Fikr-e Baleegh*.

I

Aseer-e jism hoon, miyaad-e qaid laamaaloom
Ye kis gunaah ki paadaash hai, Khuda maaloom

Teri gali to mujhe yun bhi khainchti hai bahut
Dar asl hai meri mitti kahaan ki kya maaloom

Dua karoon na karoon soch hai yehi ke tujhe
Dua ke qabl mere dil ka mudd'aa maaloom

Suni hikaayat-e hasti to darmiyaan se suni
Na ibtidaa ki khabar hai, na intihaa maaloom

Talab karein bhi to kya shai talab karein ai Shad
Hamein ko aap naheen apna mudd'aa maaloom

I

I'm my body's prisoner, how long my term, I do not know
What's my sin, what sentence, God knows, I do not know

I do not know why your lane beckons me so much
What's my soil, where's my root, I do not know

Whether I pray, or I don't, I wish you knew
What's my heart's prayer for you, I do not know

I joined the tale of life but only midway
Where it begins, where it ends, I do not know

Shad! What shall I ask for, if I ever do
What's my will, what's my wish, I do not know

2

Dhoondoge hamein mulkon mulkon, milne ke naheen naayaab
hain hum
Tabeer hai jis ki hasrat-o gham, ai ham nafaso wo khwaab
hain hum

Ai dard bataa kuchh too hi bataa, ab tak ye mu'amma hul na hua
Hum mein hai dil-e betaab nihaan, ya aap dil-e betaab hain hum

Main hairat-o hasrat ka maara, khaamosh khadaa hoon saahil pe
Daryaa-i muhabbat kehta hai, aa kuchh bhi naheen paayaab
hain hum

Ho jaai bakhedaa paak kaheen paas apne bulaa lein behtar hai
Ab dard-e judaayi se un ki ai aah bahut betaab hain hum

Lakhon hi musaafir chalte hain, manzil pe pahunchte
hain do ek
Ai ahl-e zamaana qadr karo, nayaab naheen kamyaab hain hum

Murghan-e qafas ko phulon ne ai Shad, ye kehla bheja hai
Aa jaao jo tum ko aana ho, aise mein abhi shaadaab hain hum

2

You would not find me wherever you go, rare indeed I am
My dreams take to pain and pining, such a poor dream I am

Pain, dear pain, tell me now this mystery remains a
mystery yet:
In me lies a restive heart, or a restive heart in me I am

Amazed and forlorn, I stand silent on the river's bank
Love's river calls me in: come in, a shallow bed I am

Better if the pain is over; better if she calls me now
The pangs of parting have taken a toll, so ravaged I am

Millions move to reach the goal; only a few get there at last
Value me, my dear ones; I'm not extinct, but rare I am

Shad! The blossoms have sent a message to the birds encaged:
'Come on if you may, even now a bubbly blossom I am!'

18

Hasrat Mohani

Hasrat Mohani (1875–1951) is the nom de plume of Syed Fazlul Hasan. He was born in Mohan, a *qasba* in Uttar Pradesh. After receiving his early education at home, he moved to Aligarh Muslim University from where he graduated. Hasrat realized that his forte lay both in poetry and politics, which he nursed with care and commitment. He was a nonconformist; neither a favourite of the Congress Party nor of the Muslim League, although he enjoyed a position of prestige in the Communist Party of India. He is said to have been the first champion and proclaimant of complete independence of India. He passionately worked to achieve this professed goal and was even imprisoned for his views on British rule in India and the British intervention in Egypt. He is comprehensively identified as a poet, prose writer, journalist and freedom fighter.

Hasrat was essentially a ghazal poet, who appropriated a frank and disarming idiom to reconfigure romantic love. In spite of his reservations about the ghazal, he nursed the form and proclaimed his allegiance to it. He critically appraised and drew upon the Urdu and Persian poetic traditions. His political poetry is yet another aspect where he remains almost unparalleled in acquiring an identity of his own. Hasrat was not a poet of philosophical orientation but of lighter emotions and lyric grace. He often developed narrative and dramatic strains in his ghazals, a quality that distinguished him, and brought him closer to Momin. Hasrat founded a monthly journal, *Urdu-i Mo'alla,* through which he curated and circulated the contemporary literary taste. He left behind his poetical works which were collected in thirteen volumes. Other works include his biographical notes on poets entitled *Tazkirat-us Shuaraa,* a discourse on the fine points of poetry called *Nukaat-e Sukhan,* his experiences in imprisonment put together in *Mushahidaat-e Zindaan* and a commentary on the poetry of Asadullah Khan Ghalib.

I

Hai mashq-e sukhan jaari chakki ki mushaqqat bhi
Ek turfa tamaasha hai Hasrat ki tabeeyat bhi

Jo chaahe sazaa de lo tum aur bhi khul khelo
Per hum se qasam le lo ke ho jo shikaayat bhi

Dushwaar hai rindon per inkaar-e karam yaksar
Ai saqi-i jaan parwar kuchh lutf-o-inaayat bhi

Dil bas ke hai deewaana us husn-e gulaabi ka
Rangeen hai usee roo se shaayed gham-e furqat bhi

Khud ishq ki gushtaakhi sab tujh ko sikha degi
Ai husn-e hayaa parwar shokhi bhi sharaarat bhi

Barsaat ke aate hi tauba na rahee baaqi
Baadal jo nazar aai badli meri neeyat bhi

Usshaq ke dil nazuk us shokh ki khoo nazuk
Nazuk usi nisbat se hai kaar-e muhabbat bhi

Rakhte hain mere dil per kyun tuhmat-e betaabi
Yaan nala-i muztar ki jab mujh mein ho qoowat bhi

Ai shauq ki bebaaki wo kya teri khwaahish thi
Jis per unhein ghussa hai inkaar bhi hairat bhi

Hain sad-o Safi shaair ya Shauq-o Wafa, Hasrat
Phir Zaamin-o Mahshar hain Iqbal bhi Wahshat bhi

I

He writes his verse, he grinds the stone too
That's your Hasrat, that's a rare sight too

Punish as you wish, some more if you want
I take a vow; wouldn't say a word to you

It's hard for drinkers to deny a favour
Life sustaining Saqi, be compassionate too

This heart is wild for that pink love of mine
But parting from her is colourful too

Love's ways will teach you, my coy mistress!
How to pretend, how to be naughty too

With rains, I could not sustain my abstinence
Looking at the clouds, my intentions changed too

Lovers have delicate hearts; so has she
That's how love's affair is delicate too

Why blame my heart for her impatience?
Do I have the nerve to tell my tale too?

Fearless craving! What did you crave for indeed!
That makes her angry, spurning, surprised too

Shad, Shafi are poets; Shauq, Wafa and Hasrat too
Zaamin, Mahshar also there, Iqbal and Wahshat too

2

Tujh se paas-e wafaa zaraa na hua
Hum se phir bhi tera gilaa na hua

Aise bigde ke phir jafaa bhi na kee
Dushmani ka bhi haq adaa na hua

Kuchh ajab cheez hai wo chashm-e siyah
Teer jis ka kabhi khataa na hua

Tum jafaa kaar the karam na kiya
Main wafaadaar tha khafaa na hua

Haif hai us ki baadshaahi per
Tere kooche ka jo gadaa na hua

Chhid gaee jab Jamaal-e yaar ki baat
Khatm taa der silsilaa na hua

Qaana-i ranj-e ishq tha Hasrat
Aish-e dunya se aashnaa na hua

2

You cared for love less and less
I couldn't complain of that stress

So angry, but not disloyal
Enmity's due, I did not press

How magical! Those black eyes
They shoot so straight, nonetheless

You were unfaithful, unkind
I wasn't sad, sincere no less

Many a shame on his royalty
Your lane who did not caress

When they talked of her magic
Their talking was just endless

Content with love's pain, Hasrat
The world's pleasures, he knew so less

19

Mohammad Iqbal

Mohammad Iqbal (1877–1938), a descendant of a Kashmiri Brahmin family that had embraced Islam in the seventeenth century, was born and settled in Sialkot. After a traditional education in Arabic, Persian and Urdu, he was exposed to a liberal education that defined the contours of his thought and his poetry during the entire period of his life. Beginning his educational career at the Scottish Mission School, he went on to acquire his masters degree in philosophy, before joining Trinity College, Dublin, and later earning the degree of Bar-at-Law. He furthered his education by getting a doctorate degree from Germany on *The Development of Metaphysics in Persia*. He worked in different capacities at different points of time—he taught philosophy, practised law, got involved in politics and also attended the second Round Table Conference. Even while he favoured the idea of the creation of Pakistan and is venerated there as the national poet, he wrote the famous patriotic song

'*Saare jahaan se achha Hindostan hamaaraa*' that celebrates the greatness of India. King George V knighted him after which he was known as Sir Mohammad Iqbal.

Iqbal wrote both in Persian and Urdu, and is often regarded as the poet-philosopher of the East who addressed the Muslim *ummah*, believed in the philosophy of *wahdat-ul wujood*, or unity of being, and propounded the philosophy of *khudi*, or selfhood, which called for self-realization and the discovery of the hidden talent with love and perseverance. Beyond that lay the stages of complete submission and forgetfulness which, he thought, was the ultimate stage of *khudi*. Iqbal dreamt of the 'complete man' and entered into a metaphoric dialogue with the divine. His poetry emerged as a remarkable site where social commentary and art coalesced, as he reconfigured major poetic devices like the metaphor, renewed the use of myth and symbolism to revisit history, philosophy and the Islamic faith to develop his individual vision. He has left behind his collections of poems, *Asraar-e Khudi, Rumooz-e Bekhudi, Baang-e Daraa, Baal-e Jibreel, Payaam-e Mashriq, Zaboor-e Ajm, Javed Naama, Zarb-e Kaleem,* and *Armaghaan-e Hijaz,* apart from his lectures collected in English as *The Reconstruction of Religious Thought in Islam,* and other works on the Eastern world-view.

I

Sitaaron se aage jahaan aur bhee hain
Abhi ishq ke imtihaan aur bhee hain

Tahi zindagi se naheen ye fizaaein
Yahaan saikadon karwaan aur bhee hain

Qanaa'at na kar aalam-e rang-o boo per
Chaman aur bhi aashiyaan aur bhee hain

Agar kho gaya ik nasheman to gham kyaa
Maqaamaat-e aah-o fughaan aur bhee hain

Tu shaheen hai parwaaz hai kaam tera
Tere saamne aasmaan aur bhee hain

Isee roz-o shab mein ulajh kar na rah jaa
Ke tere zamaan-o makaan aur bhee hain

Gaye din ke tanhaa tha mein anjuman mein
Yahaan ab mere raazdaan aur bhee hain

I

Beyond the stars, many a world
Before love is proved, many a test

The space, not shorn of blessings
Moving about, many a caravan

No end to the world of glamour
Many a garden, many a nest

Why worry, if an abode is lost
For my laments, many a space

You, a falcon, for you a flight
Many a sky, many a cloud

Don't be snared by days and nights
You've many a time, many a place

No more a stranger, here and now
I've many a keeper, many a kin

2

Agar kaj rau hain anjum aasmaan teraa hai ya meraa
Mujhe fikr-e jahaan kyun ho jahaan teraa hai ya meraa

Agar hangaama-hai shauq se hai laamakaan khaali
Khataa kis ki hai ya Rub! Laamakaan teraa hai ya meraa

Use subh-e azal inkaar ki jur'at huee kyunkar
Mujhe maloom kya, wo raazdaan teraa hai ya meraa

Muhammad bhi tera, Jibreel bhi, Qur'an bhi teraa
Magar ye harf-e shireen tarjumaan teraa hai ya meraa

Usee kaukab ki taabani se hai teraa jahaan raushan
Zawaal-e Aadam-e khaaki ziyaan teraa hai ya meraa

2

If the stars waver, whose sky is that? Yours or mine?
Why should I worry, whose world is this? Yours or mine?

If the sphere is devoid of all its hum and buzz
Whose fault, my God? Whose sphere is that? Yours or mine?

How could he get courage to deny the first dawn?
How do I know, whose confidante is he? Yours or mine?

Muhammad yours, Gabriel yours, yours the Holy Book
But those sweet words? Whose intents are those? Yours or mine?

That shining star keeps your world aglow for ever
Whose loss, the fall of the earthly Adam? Yours or mine?

20

Fani Badayuni

Fani Badayuni (1879–1941) is the nom de plume of Shaukat Ali Khan, who was born in Badayun, Uttar Pradesh. His ancestors had migrated to India from Kabul during the reign of Shah Alam II, and enjoyed a high status with a huge estate to their credit. Following his education in traditional disciplines and languages, Fani studied law but did not find it interesting enough to pursue as a career. Although his father had advised him to keep away from poetry that was merely imaginative and unproductive, he continued his affair with the muse in secrecy and wrote both in Persian and Urdu. Later, he migrated to Hyderabad, took up an appointment as a teacher but could not continue with it for long. He died there, unhappy and disappointed with life generally. Genuine and warm at heart, he lived with his uncompromising pride and preferred suffering to mindless submission.

Mystical contemplation and romantic despair are the two major markers of Fani's experiential capital. His perception of the tragic distinguished him as a philosopher of pain, and his perception of the artistic defined him as a poet. His poetry is replete with pain and pining, which he expressed with remarkable sincerity. His personal disappointments had brought him closer to the understanding of suffering in life. He did not believe in the notion of art for life's sake, as he laid greater emphasis on poetry as a serious literary vocation. He was very conscious of the tools and techniques of poetry, and was given wholly to crafting his poetry as an example of high art. His poetry is marked also for its conversational idiom and dialogic nature. Fani made his place in the literary canon slowly and painfully, just as he found his own life passing rather slowly and painfully. The several volumes of his poetry have been collected together in *Kulliyaat-e Fani*.

I

Jee dhoondta hai ghar koee dono jahaan se door
Is aap ki zameen se alag aasmaan se door

Shaayad main dar khure nigah-e garm bhi naheen
Bijlee tadap rahi hai meri aashiyaan se door

Wo poochte hain aur koee deta naheen jawaab
Kis ki wafaa hai dastaras-e imtihaan se door

Aankhein churaa ke aap ne afsaana kar diya
Jo haal tha zubaan se qareeb aur bayaan se door

Hai man'a raah-e ishq mein dair-o haram ka hosh
Yaani kahaan se paas hai manzil kahaan se door

Ta arz-e shauq mein na rahe bandagee ki laag
Ek sajda chaahta hoon tere aastaan se door

Fani Dakan mein aa ke ye uqda khulaa ke hum
Hindostaan mein rahte hain Hindostaan se door

I

I look for a home away from both the worlds, far away
Away from this earth of yours, from the skies, far away

I am not the favoured one, not even of the fiery looks
The lightening shows, away from my abode, so very far away

No one gives an answer; he only keeps on asking all
Whose love defies a test, whose love hides, so far away

When you turned your eyes, you helped a story go afloat
That was a tale close to tongue but from telling, far away

In love, who cares where the temple is, where the mosque
Does it matter if the goal is near, or at distant, far away

So that there is no trace of my devotion in my imploring
I only wish I could bow my head, from your abode, far away

Fani! It was only in the far off Deccan, I got to know
I lived in Hindostaan but from Hindostaan, far away

2

Har saans ke saath jaa rahaa hoon
Main tere qareeb aa rahaa hoon

Ye dil mein karaahne lagaa kaun
Ro ro ke kise rulaa rahaa hoon

Ab 'ishq ko beneqaab kar ke
Main husn ko aazmaa rahaa hoon

Asraar-e jamaal khul rahe hain
hastee ka suraagh paa rahaa hoon

Tanhaa-i sham-e ghum ke dar se
Kuchh un se jawaab paa rahaa hoon

Lazzat kashe-e aarzoo hoon Fani
Danista fareb khaa rahaa hoon

2

I pass away with every passing breath
I reach you with every passing breath

Who moans within my heart, who
With my cries, I make the other cry too

Unveiling the love at last
I test my own love at last

The secrets of beauty unravel
Through the routes of being I travel

I fear the lonesomeness of painful nights
I get her answers for those baleful nights

Fani, I enjoy when I crave
What deceptions I do brave!

2 I

Asghar Gondawi

Asghar Gondawi (1884–1936) is the *nome de plume* of Asghar Hussain who was born in Gorakhpur. As he hailed from a family of limited economic means, he could not get conventional education but made personal efforts to study Urdu, Arabic, Persian and English. He worked for Urdu Markaz, the centre for Urdu writers and Urdu lovers in Lahore, but could not continue there for long. Later, he joined Tej Bahadur Sapru's Hindustani Press in Allahabad as an editor.

Asghar had a philosophical disposition which clearly marks the major part of his poetry. In his earlier phase, he wrote under the influence of Sufi poets. However, later, he acquired a personal tone and tenor which no other poet of mystical nature could achieve after him. His poetry is characterized by a soft, melancholic voice that highlighted his ability to think metaphysically and render his thoughts with poetic credibility. Asghar was not a prolific poet, as he was more preoccupied with the idea of artistic merit which was manifested in his ability to rethink the stock romantic metaphors and appropriate them in both romantic and spiritualist ghazals. The thematic richness and artistic control of his voice are discernible in his collections, *Nishat-e Rooh* and *Surood-e Zindagi*.

I

Tamaam daftar-e hikmat ulat gaya hoon mein
Magar khulaa na abhi tak kahaan hoon, kya hoon main

Ye mujh se poochhiye kya guftugoo mein lazzat hai
Fiza-i dehr mein tehleel ho gaya hoon main

Kabhi khayaal ke hai khwaab aalam-e hastee
Zameer mein abhi fitrat ke, so raha hoon main

Kabhi ye fakhr ke aalam mein aks hai meraa
Khud apnaa tarz-e nazar hai ke dekhta hoon main

Hayaat-o maut bhi adnaa si ek kadi meri
Azal se le ke abad tak wo silsila hoon main

Nawaa-i raaz ka seene mein khoon hotaa hai
Sitam hai, lafz paraston mein ghir gaya hoon main

Na koee naam hai mera, na koee soorat hai
Kuchh is tarah hama tan deed ho gaya hoon main

Tera jamaal hai, tera khayaal hai, too hai
Mujhe ye fursat-e kaawish kahaan ke kya hoon main

I

I've ransacked the seas of wisdom, don't know where I am
I don't know even now: who I am, where I am

Ask me what's pleasure talking, I'll tell you what:
That's melting in timeless time, that's being where I am

This state of being is only a dream, I think at times
Slumbering long in nature's conscience, that's where I am

That the world bears my image, often makes me proud
That's how I see myself, that's indeed where I am

Life and death, the two links in the long chain of life
And I in a flux from end to end, that's where I am

My secret voices meet their death, buried in the breast
I'm trapped among wordsmiths! It's a pity, where I am

Neither a name, nor a face; I have none of mine
All askance, body and soul, that's what and where I am

Your elegance, your thought, your being: that's all I know
Not a while to know more: who I am, where I am

2

Bistar-e khaak pe baithha hoon na masti hai, na hosh
Zarre sab saakit-o saamit hain, sitaare khaamosh

Nazar aati hai mazaahir mein meri shakl mujhe
Fitrat aaeena badast aur main hairaan-o khamosh

Tarjumaani ki mujhe aaj ijaazat de de
Shajar-e toor hai saakit, lab-e Mansoor khamosh

Partaw-e mehr hi zauq-e rum-o bedaari de
Bistar-e gul pe hai ek qatra-i shabnam khaamosh

2

I'm in the earth's cradle, neither in senses nor in elation
Each particle of dust at rest, each star silent

I can see my face in countless images around
Nature holds a mirror to me; I'm stunned and silent

Let me tell you the truth today, let me tell you now:
Toor's branch is all still, Mansoor's lips are all silent

Love's face may alone revive the life of my senses
On the bed of blossoms, lies a drop of dew silent

22

Yaas Yagana Changezi

Yaas Yagana Changezi (1884–1956), whose ancestors had migrated from Iran and joined the Mughal army, was born in Azimabad, now Patna, and named Mirza Wajid Hussain. He also wrote under the pen name of 'Yaas' (despair) before choosing 'Yagana' (matchless) as his nom de plume. This choice for a change of name reflected his independent and defiant nature. Shad Azimabadi, another major poet who lived in Azimabad, pruned his taste and helped him hone his talent. Yagana shifted to Calcutta and got married there, but chose to find a new home in Lucknow, only to discover to his utter despair that the place was unkind to him. As he was egotistical, uncompromising and unable to control his brusque manners and speech, he could not strike a chord with the poets there. He caused controversies and came to be identified as a highly nonconformist, controversial and provocative poet, who found faults even with Asadulla Khan Ghalib and Mohammed Iqbal.

He even went to the extent of making controversial statements about religious belief and was once attacked by a mob.

Quite in keeping with his personality, Yagana's tone in his poetry was direct, curt and stinging but he was sober and dignified in his renditions despite his iconoclasm. More than writing about the myriad manifestations of love, he wrote about the manifestations of life in his poetry. He developed a brave and bold attitude towards life and the dignity of man even while he engaged with the oddities of life uncompromisingly. A certain sense of scepticism that took over him did not allow him to achieve a broader philosophical stance in his poetry. Yagana was essentially an interrogator of both life and art, who lived and survived in his individual splendour. Yagana's works are collected in *Nashtar-e Yas, Taraana, Aayaat-e Wijdaani* and *Ganjeena*.

I

Kaargaah-e dunya mein neesti bhi hasti hai
Ek taraf ujadti hai aik samt basti hai

Bedilon ki hasti kya jeete hain na marte hain
Khwab hai na bedaari hosh hai na masti hai

Kya bataoon kya hoom main qudrat-e Khuda hoon main
Meri khud parasti bhi 'ain haq parasti hai

Keemiya-i dil kya hai khaak hai magar kaisi
Lijiye to mehngi hai bechiye to sasti hai

Khizr-e manzil apna hoon apni raah chalta hoon
Mere haal per dunya kya samajh ke hansti hai

Kya kahoon safar apna khatm kyun naheen hota
Fikr ki balandi ya hausle ki pasti hai

Husn-e betamaasha ki dhoom kya muamma hai
Kaan bhi hain namahram aankh bhi tarasti hai

Chitwanon se milta hai kuchh suragh baatin ka
Chaal se to kafir per saadagi barasti hai

Tark-e lazzat-e dunya kijiye to kis dil se
Zauq-e paarsaayi kya faiz-e tang dastee hai

Deedani hai Yaas apne ranj-o-ghum ki tughyaani
Jhoom jhoom kar kya kya ye ghata barasti hai

I

The ruins of the world are life's share
Some perish here, some prosper there

The heartless ones neither live nor die
Nor drink, nor sink, nor sing, nor sigh

I'm God's miracle, no more, no less
I love Him, I love myself no less

Heart's alchemy, what worth, what mould
Costly if bought, cheap if sold

My own guide, I walk my way to goal
None should laugh at me, none should cajole

What's the matter, why don't I arrive?
Do I sink low, or never strive?

What a puzzle is that naive love indeed!
Ears await her words, eyes askance indeed

The face tells what surely lies inside
Though her manners don't at all abide

How can one renounce this world's pleasures?
Is piety a gift of living in measures

My pain's ebb and flow worth a watch, Yaas
The dark clouds bring in torrents, alas!

2

Kis ki aawaaz kaan mein aaee
Door ki baat dhyaan mein aaee

Aap aate rahe bulaate rahe
Aane waali ik aan mein aaee

Ye kinaara chalaa ke naao chali
Kahiye kya baat dhyaan mein aaee

'Ilm kya 'ilm ki haqeeqat kyaa
Jaisi jis ke gumaan mein aaee

Aankh neechi huee arey ye kyaa
Yoon gharaz darmiyaan mein aaee

Main payamber naheen Yagana sahi
Is se kyaa kasr shaan mein aaee

2

Whose voice? What did I hear?
A distant thought brought me cheer

All entreating but only a trash
One meant to come, came in a flash

Is the bank moving, or is it the boat?
Say, what thought is now afloat?

What is knowledge, what is its worth?
We had aplenty, there was no dearth

Your eyes downcast, what's the matter?
A selfish motive, enough to shatter

I'm only Yagana, not God's envoy
But why should that ever annoy

23

Jigar Moradabadi

Jigar Moradabadi (1890–1960) is the nom de plume of Ali Sikandar, who was born in Moradabad and settled in Gonda. He was not educated formally but learnt Arabic, Urdu and Persian at a madrasa. Asghar Gondawi, a poet of renown, played a significant role in his life, both as a mentor and a friend. Jigar represented the iconic figure of a romantic Urdu poet who had developed a certain aura about his personality, was drunk to the brim, and performed in the mushairas on the strength of his sonorous voice. In his ghazals, Jigar took to eulogizing wine, beauty and love to the ultimate stage. It was only towards the end of his life that he distanced himself from alcohol and drew close to mysticism, which is reflected in his later poetry.

Although shorn of philosophical depth, Jigar's ghazals remained a measure of what ghazal as a form stood for. He emerged as a very popular poet, of the common masses as well as the literary readers, who celebrated the joys of life and the buoyancy of youth by drawing upon stock images and metaphors of Persian and Urdu poetry. He kept away from the complex and heavily Persianized turns of phrases, as he brought poetry closer to common parlance. His appeal lay in the simplicity of his diction, the rhythmic nature of his verse, and the easy accessibility he offered to his uniquely epicurean world. *Daagh-e Jigar, Shola-i Toor,* and *Aatish-e Gul,* for which he got the Sahitya Akademi award, are his three collections.

I

Koee ye keh de gulshan gulshan
Laakh balaaein ek nasheman

Kaamil rahbar qaatil rahzan
Dil saa dost na dil saa dushman

Phool khile hain gulshan gulshan
Lekin apna apna daaman

Hasti-i shaair Allah Allah
Husn ki manzil ishq ka madfan

Rangeen fitrat saada tabeeyat
Farsh nasheen aur arsh nasheman

Kaam adhooraa aur aazaadi
Naam bade aur thode darshan

Shama hai lekin dhundli dhundli
Saaya hai lekin raushan raushan

Kaanton ka bhi haq hai kuchh aakhir
Kaun chhudaai apna daaman

Chalti phirti chhaaon hai pyare
Kis ka sehra kaisa gulshan

I

A word be heard in meadows, boroughs
Enough a home for many sorrows

Heart, a cruel robber, a perfect guide
And heart: a friend, a foe, a pride

Many a bliss from place to place
To each one a grace, a disgrace

Poet's being in full bloom
Beauty's goal, love's tomb

Radiant nature, simple at best
Earth an abode, sky a nest

All freedom, little deeds
Big names, little proceeds

The lamp burns dim and light
But the shadows all bright

Thorns lay their own barb
Who can save one's own garb

All of them, passing shadows
Wilds, bowers and meadows

2

Saqi ki har nigaah pe bal kha ke pee gayaa
Lehron se kheltaa hua lehra ke pee gayaa

Bekaifiyon ke kaif se ghabra ke pee gayaa
Tauba ko tod taad ke ghabra ke pee gayaa

Zaahid ye teri shokhi-i rindaana dekhnaa
Rahmat ko baaton baaton mein behla ke pee gayaa

Sarmasti-i azal jo mujhe yaad aa gaye
Dunyaa-i aitabaar ko thhukra ke pee gayaa

Aazurdag-i khaatir-e saqi ko dekh kar
Mujhko ye sharm aaee ke sharma ke pee gayaa

Ai rahmat-e tamaam, meri har khataa mu'aaf
Mein intihaa-i shauq mein ghabra ke pee gayaa

Peeta beghair izn ye kab thee meri majaal
Dar parda chashm-e yaar ki shah paa ke pee gayaa

Us jan-e maikada ki qasam baarhaa Jigar
Kul aalam-e baseet pe mein chha ke pee gayaa

2

I watched the Saqi's gaze each time I drank my drink
I played with waves, I danced with them, I drank my drink

Nervous at the elation of boredom, I drank my drink
I broke the promise of abstinence, I drank my drink

O devout one, that's your real drinker's courage
You took in nature's bounty well, I drank my drink

When I recalled the bliss and boon of eternity
I kicked the bubbling world aside, I drank my drink

The Saqi was sorrowful, I too watched his gloom
I felt ashamed; in sheer shame, I drank my drink

O kindness incarnate! Forgive my failings for now
In pure delight, I got unnerved, I drank my drink

How could I drink without a nod, without courage?
But my dear love gave me a nod, I drank my drink

I swear by the one who rules the tavern, Jigar
Many a time, I ruled the world, I drank my drink

24

Firaq Gorakhpuri

Firaq Gorakhpuri (1896–1982), born Raghupati Sahay, acquired a taste for poetry from his father, Munshi Gorakh Prasad Ibrat, who practised law and wrote poetry of classical temper. Firaq began his education with learning the Urdu language, which ultimately became the chosen medium of his poetic expression. After his early education, he moved to Allahabad for higher education at Muir Inter College. He was selected for the job of a deputy collector but he declined the offer. Instead, he joined India's freedom movement and was imprisoned, like others, for his anti-British activities. On release from prison, he taught at Christian College, Lucknow, and then at Sanatan Dharm College, Kanpur. Later, he got his master's degree in English literature, and joined Allahabad University as a faculty member. Firaq was much honoured as a poet and was decorated with the highest literary award, the Jnanpith. He was the first recipient of this award for a work written in the Urdu language.

The blessings of romantic love and sex, human yearnings, life's incongruities and the mysteries of the dark night engaged him incessantly in his poetry. He drew upon the Hindu mythology on the one hand, and the Hindi and Sanskrit idiom on the other. In doing this, he found space for pan-Indian thoughts and feelings in his poetry, as also a way to impart a new tone and tenor to the Urdu idiom. Some of his critics believe that his tone and tenor did not match with the genius of the Urdu language and the Persian-Urdu sensibility. Firaq also drew upon other poets of the classical Hindi and Sanskrit traditions like Surdas, Kalidas and Kabir, as well as of the English Romantic poets of the early nineteenth century, apart from the Urdu poet, Sheikh Ghulam Ali Hamadani Mus'hafi. Firaq spoke in soft, subdued and delicate tones to configure the delicacy and exquisiteness of love and the figure of the beloved. He was also a critic of the impressionistic style of poetry writing. His poetry collections include *Naghma-i Saaz*, *Ghazalistaan*, *Sheristaan*, *Shabnamistaan*, *Roo-e Kainat*, *Gul-e Naghma*, *Dharti ki Karwat*, *Gul-e Barg*, and *Roop*, a collection of *rubais*, the four-line metrical compositions.

I

Sukoot-e shaam mitaao bahut andheraa hai
Sukhan ki shama jalaao bahut andheraa hai

Dayaar-e ghum mein dil-e beqaraar chhoot gaya
Sambhal ke dhoondne jaao bahut andheraa hai

Ye raat wo hai ke soojhe jahaan na haath ko haath
Khayaalo door na jaao bahut andheraa hai

Laton ko chehre pe daale wo so rahaa hai kaheen
Zayaa-i rukh ko churaao bahut andheraa hai

Shab-e siyaah mein gum ho gaee hai raah-e hayaat
Qadam sambhal ke uthhaao bahut andheraa hai

Guzishta 'ahd ki yaadon ko phir karo taaza
Bujhe chiraagh jalaao bahut andheraa hai

Thee ek uchti hui neend zindagi us ki
Firaq ko na jagaao bahut andheraa hai

I

Let not the quiet of dusk grow, it's too dark
Let the flames of words glow, it's too dark

Left behind in pain's country, my impatient heart
Be careful when you trace tomorrow, it's too dark

Such a dark night! A hand cannot see a hand
Don't go too far, dear thoughts; don't go, it's too dark

With her tresses spread around, she lies asleep
Steal the flame of a face in glow, it's too dark

It's a dark night, I cannot find life's trail
Move with care when you wish to go, it's too dark

Light up the slumbering memories of past now
Bring the silent lamps back to glow, it's too dark

His life was a slumber; he slumbered only in parts
Let Firaq be asleep; let him be so, it's too dark

2

Raat bhi neend bhi kahaani bhi
Hai kyaa cheez hai jawaani bhi

Ek paigham-e zindagaani bhi
Aashiqi marg-e naagahaani bhi

Is adaa ka teri jawaab naheen
Mehrabaani bhi sargaraani bhi

Dil ko apne bhi gham the dunya mein
Kuchh balaaein theen aasmaani bhi

Dil ko sholon se karti hai sairaab
Zindagi aag bhi hai paani bhi

Ishq-e naakaam ki hai parchhaaeen
Shaadmaani bhi kaamraani bhi

Khalq kyaa kyaa mujhe naheen kehtee
kuchh sunoon main teri zabaani bhi

Dil-e badnaam tere baare mein
Log kahte hain ek kahaani bhi

Zindagi ain deed-e yaar Firaq
Zindagi hijr ki kahaani bhi

2

A night, slumber, a tale too
Pure bliss, bubbly life's ale too

Love, the message of life but
It's a sudden death's wail too

Just no match to ways of love
A kind and unkind veil too

A heart and the pain of the heart
Curse of divine scale too

A heart, wet with blazing flames
Life is water, fire's trail too

Shadows of a love that failed
A pleasure, a victory's trail too

The world treasures my tale now
Now, let me hear its tale too

For my ill-reputed heart
The world sure has a tale too

Life, a look of love, Firaq
But a parting's sad tale too

PROGRESSIVE POETICS

The Progressive Writers Movement that brought together a group of poets in the 1930s marked a clear rejection of romantic ideals in poetry and poetics. Contemporary Indian and world events provided the progressive poets their immediate context. It lay in the general decadence of the socio-political condition of India and the world during the 1930s, India's struggle for independence, the dawn of a new India following its 'tryst with destiny', and the prospects of India emerging as a nation state with adequate space for social, economic and political justice. In literature, it chronicled the major marks of a historical period in turmoil and a political order in disarray. The movement sought its inspiration from the Soviet writers and their ways of negotiating with contemporary crisis. The philosophers of the movement made a radical statement in their manifesto against the prevailing decadence in life and literature. They gave a clarion call for reason against sentimentality, realism against romance, and freedom against subjugation. At the social level, they rejected the feudal order and decadent morality; at the political level, they sought recourse to leftist ideology; and in the domain of literature, they made an organized effort to refute and resist the centuries-old romantic-spiritualist tradition, which they considered to be a way of escaping the stark realities of contemporary life. Aiming at socio-political rejuvenation, they called for dismantling all retrograde institutions surviving under the unchallenged authority of tradition and coercive power. Being anti-imperialist in nature, they fostered the spirit of decolonization, called for India's independence, and brought people face-to-face with the general human condition characterized by insecurity, oppression, loss and despair at all levels. Thus, the Progressive poetics disengaged from clichés of all sorts and romantic exuberance of all kinds. Charged with Marxist ideology, it resisted social, political, cultural and literary establishments and stereotypes. With a clear commitment to a certain kind of poetry, the Progressive poets and writers sought their inspiration from diverse quarters—indigenous and foreign, as also literary and extra-literary. Even though they firmly believed in their sacrosanct manifesto, some of them saw it failing in the face of art. The movement, however, continued propagating the gospel of art for life's sake, parallel to another group of poets who came together under the banner of Halqa-i Arbab-e Zauq, the circle of connoisseurs, who advocated the idea of art for art's sake.

25

Asrarul Haq Majaz

Asrarul Haq Majaz (1909–1955) was born in Rudauli, a *qasba* in Uttar Pradesh. After his early education at home, he moved to Lucknow, then Agra for further education, and finally to Aligarh from where he got his bachelor's degree. It was during his stay at Aligarh that the Progressive Writers Movement had started taking root in the imagination of the socially conscious poets and writers. Impressed by the aims of this Movement, he joined it with enthusiasm. He also wrote the *taraana*, the anthem, for Aligarh Muslim University which is sung there with great fervour. Later, he worked for the All India Radio, Delhi; the Ministry of Information in Maharashtra, Bombay; Harding Public Library, Delhi; and *Naya Adab*, Lucknow. A depressed alcoholic, Majaz suffered a mental breakdown and died in a tavern in Lucknow, the city whose name he had appended with his own to be called Majaz Lucknowi.

Majaz was deeply moved by the decadent socio-political order of his times. He thought that the Progressive Writers Movement would provide a panacea, but realized later that literature could not survive with slogans or lofty ideals alone; it had to be artistically mature. He then came to address more perennial issues in his works than topical ones. He reflected upon universal human sentiments, combined the personal with the social, and the social with the political, in an artful manner to make his poetry and prose appealing and lasting. Majaz also wrote romantic poems. Although he had begun traditionally— by composing ghazals, he moved on to nazm, or the regular poem, later, which gave him greater scope to engage with the issues of contemporary relevance and personal dilemmas. His works are collected in *Aahang, Shab-e Taab*, and *Saaz-e Nau*, an anthology of stories.

I

Barbaad-e tamanna pe ataab aur ziyaada
Haan meri mohabbat ka jawaab aur ziyaada

Roein na abhi ahl-e nazar haal pe mere
Hona hai abhi mujh ko kharaab aur ziyaada

Aawaara-o majnoon pe hi mauqoof nahi kuchh
Milne hain abhi mujh ko khitaab aur ziyaada

Uthhenge abhi aur bhi toofaan mere dil se
Dekhunga abhi ishq ke khwaab aur ziyaada

Tapkega lahu aur mere dida-i tar se
Dhadkega dil-khaana kharaab aur ziyaada

Hogi meri baton se unhein aur bhi hairat
Aaiga unhein mujh se hijaab aur ziyaada

Ai mutrib-e bebaak koee aur bhi naghma
Ai Saqi-i fayyaz sharaab aur ziyaada

I

Let the lovesick be distressed, a little more
Yes, more returns for my love, a little more

Let not the wise ones shed tears on me
I am destined to be ruined, a little more

Not only lovesick shall I be called
I shall get other catcalls, a little more

Many more tumults shall rise from my heart
I shall dream of tumultuous love, a little more

Some more blood shall then drop from my eyes
My spoilt heart shall then beat, a little more

She would be much more surprised at my words
She would then grow shy with me, a little more

Fearless singer! Sing me another song
Generous Saqi! Pour me a drink, a little more

2

Jigar aur dil ko bachaanaa bhi hai
Nazar aap hi se milaanaa bhi hai

Muhabbat ka har bhed paanaa bhi hai
Magar apna daaman bachaanaa bhi hai

Jo dil tere gham ka nishaanaa bhi hai
Qateel-e jafaa-i zamaanaa bhi hai

Ye bijli chamakti hai kyun dam ba dam
Chaman mein koee aashiyaanaa bhi hai

Khirad ki ataa'at zuroori sahi
Yehi to junoon ka zamaanaa bhi hai

Na duniya, na 'uqba kahaan jaaeeye
Kaheen ahl-e dil ka thhikaanaa bhi hai

Mujhe aaj sahil pe rone bhi do
Ke toofaan main muskuraanaa bhi hai

Zamaane se aage to badhiye Majaz
Zamaane ko aage badhaanaa bhi hai

2

My heart, my soul, I must also save
But our two glances must also meet

Love's each secret, I must also get
My esteem too, I must also keep

My heart, the victim of all the pains
Time's poor victim, it must also be

Why this lightning? So now and then
Isn't there a nest? There must also be

The call of reason must get a heed
But the wild times must also live

Not here, not hereafter—where then?
A lovers' home, there must also be

Let me shed tears on this riverbank
But in the tides' grip, I must also be

Go ahead of the times, Majaz, go
The world and the time must also move

26

Faiz Ahmad Faiz

Faiz Ahmad Faiz (1911–1984), poet, academic, army personnel, journalist and political activist, was born in Sialkot and educated in Lahore. After learning his Urdu and Persian, he studied English and Arabic for his master's degree. He started his career as a lecturer in English but relinquished his job during World War II to join the British Indian Army. He attained the rank of Lt Colonel and received an MBE for his war-time services. After the Partition of India, he worked as editor of the daily, *The Pakistan Times* and the weekly, *Lail-o Nahaar*. He was also imprisoned in connection with the Rawalpindi Conspiracy Case. Later, he spent several years in Lebanon editing *Lotus*, an international leftist magazine. He returned to Pakistan at the fag end of his career in 1984, and died the same year in Lahore.

A torchbearer of the Progressive Writers Movement and a committed Marxist, Faiz was one of the few poets to strike a delicate balance between arts and ideas and emerge as an icon.

He was a votary of free expression, democratic values and a world order based on socio-political justice. The stages of his development show how his craft matured—from romanticism to social realism, and then to a deeper awareness of the larger human predicament. Faiz exploited the traditional symbols of Persian and Urdu poetry to add new implications to them and broaden the frontiers of meaning. He blended tradition with modernity and evolved a rare sense of the musical, which distinguished his poetry and attracted a huge mass of readers and musicians to his works. Faiz has remained a potent influence on his contemporaries and on younger generations. He received many awards, including the Lenin Peace Prize, awarded by the Soviet government. Collections of his poetry include *Naqsh-e Faryaadi, Dast-e Sabaa, Zindaan Namah, Dast-e Tah-e Sang, Sar-e Wad-i Seena, Mere Dil Mere Musaafir* and *Saare Sukhan Hamaare*. Faiz is the most frequently translated of the Urdu poets in English, apart from many other languages from all over the world.

I

Aai kuchh abr kuchh sharaab aai
Us ke baad aai jo 'azaab aai

Baam-e meena se aaftaab utre
Dast-e Saqi mein maahtaab aai

Har rag-e khoon mein phir charaghaan ho
Saamne phir wo benaqaab aai

Kar raha tha gham-e jahaan ka hisaab
Aaj tum yaad behisaab aai

Na gaee teri gham ki sardaari
Dil mein yoon roz inquilaab aai

Is tarah apni khaamshi goonji
Goya har samt se jawaab aai

Faiz thee raah sar ba sar manzil
Hum jahaan pahunche kaamyaab aai

I

Let some clouds gather, let some wine flow
Then come what may when I'm all aglow

Let the sun descend the wine vessel
On Saqi's palm, let the moonshine glow

Let each vein aglow with lamplight
Let the lover's face without a veil show

I sat to count all life's loss and gain
Your memories came, all in a row

Your sorrows would rule the day ever
Though many upheavals I would know

My silence resounded, as it did
Each direction sent back an echo

Faiz! My path is surely my goal
I meet success wherever I go

2

Bedum hue beemaar dawaa kyun naheen dete
Tum achhe maseehaa ho shafaa kyun naheen dete

Dard-e shab-e hijraan ki jazaa kyun naheen dete
Khoon-e dil-e wahshi ka silaa kyun naheen dete

Mit jaaegi makhlooq to insaaf karoge
Munsif ho to ab hashr uthhaa kyun naheen dete

Haan nukta waro laao lab-o dil ki gawaahee
Haan naghma garo, saaz-e sadaa kyun naheen dete

Paimaan-e junoon haathon ko sharmaaiga kab tak
Dil walo garebaan ka pataa kyun naheen dete

Barbaad-i ye dil jabr naheen, Faiz kisee kaa
Wo dushman-e jaan hai to bhulaa kyun naheen dete

2

The sick are miserable, why don't you give them a cure
You are a good messiah, why don't you give them a cure?

For the sad nights of parting, why don't you give a reward?
For the slaughter of wild hearts, why don't you bring a gift?

When will you give verdict? After the living will perish?
If a real judge, why don't you pronounce a doomsday?

Yes, my friends, let our lips and hearts stand witness
Yes, my music makers, why don't you sing to a fine tune

How long would the hands be ashamed for not meeting their
vows
Brave hearts, why don't you ask to catch them by their collars?

Faiz, why should anyone be wrecked and ruined in love?
If that's an unkind love, why don't you simply abjure?

27

Moin Ahsan Jazbi

Moin Ahsan Jazbi (1912–2005) was born in Mubarakpur, a
qasba in Azamgarh, Uttar Pradesh. He received his education
in several places that include Jhansi, Lucknow, Agra, Delhi
and Aligarh. He got his MA and PhD degrees from Aligarh
Muslim University. He began his career as an assistant editor
of *Ajkal* (Delhi) but resigned later to take up a faculty position
at Aligarh Muslim University, where he stayed all through.

Like other poets of his time, Jazbi too was influenced by
the Progressive Writers Movement. He wrote poems on the
common themes of suffering that had engaged the attention
of every writer during that time. Realizing the limitations of
such writing, he saved his poetry from turning propagandist,
as he came to believe that poetry had to be written with a
greater sense of discrimination, and not merely to raise
an issue. His revised the traditional modes of thought and
expression in his ghazals to make way for the expression of a

new consciousness in a new language. *Farozaan* and *Sukhan Mukhtasar* are his two collections of poems. These are put together in *Kulliyaat-e Jazbi*.

I

Marne ki duaa'ein kyun maangoon, jine ki tamannaa kaun kare
Ye dunya ho yaa wo dunya, ab khwaahish-e dunyaa kaun kare

Jab kashti saabit-o-saalim thee, saahil ki tamannaa kis ko thee
Ab aisi shikasta kashti per saahil ki tamanna kaun kare

Jo aag lagaaee thee tum ne us ko to bujhaaya ashkon nein
Jo ashkon ne bhadkaayi hai us aag ko thandaa kaun kare

Dunya ne hamein chhodaa Jazbi, hum chhod na dein kyun dunya ko
Dunya ko samajh kar baithhe hain, ab dunya dunyaa kaun kare

I

Why should I pray for death, why should I worry for life?
Be it this or that world, why should I care for any?

Who wished to reach the shore, when the boat was all intact?
With a shattered boat now, why should I care for the shore?

The fire you started once, tears have put that fire out
But the fire raised by tears, who would put that fire out?

The world deserted me, Jazbi, why shouldn't I desert the world?
I have known it well, why should I pine for the world now?

2

Beete hue dinon ki hilaawat kahaan se laaein
Ek meethhe meethhe dard ki raahat kahaan se laaein

Dhoonde kahaan wo nala-i shab taab ka jamaal
Aah-e sehar gahi ki sabaahat kahaan se laaein

Samjhaaein kaise dil ki nazaakat kaa maajra
Khamoshi-i nazar ki khitaabat kahaan se laaein

Tark-e ta'alluqaat ka ho jis se ihtemaal
Be baakiyon mein itni sadaaqat kahaan se laaein

Afsurdagi-i zabt-e alam aaj bhi sahi
Lekin nishaat-e zabt-e musarrat kahaan se laaein

Har fat'ha ke ghuroor mein bewaj'ha besabab
Ehsaas-e infa'aal-e hazeemat kahaan se laaein

Asoodagi-i lutf-o inaayat ke saath saath
Dil mein dabi dabi si qayaamat kahaan se laaein

Wo josh-e iztaraab pe kuchh sochne ke baad
Hairat kahaan se laaein nadaamat kahaan se laaein

2

The bliss of the days gone by, where shall I get now?
The pleasures of a sweet pain, where shall I get now?

Where shall I find the beauty of the radiant nights?
The grace of the dawn's moaning, where shall I get now?

How shall I describe what a fragile heart I have?
The magic of a quiet glance, where shall I get now?

The fear of parting ways that lurks around ever
That truth of artful daring, where shall I get now?

The sorrow of bearing pain lives on even today
But the delight of bearing pleasure, where shall I get now?

In the vain pride of each victory for no reason
The sense of shame on each defeat, where shall I get now?

With that rare contentment drawn from love and care
A torment hidden in the heart, where shall I get now?

After sparing a thought on my effusive ways
That very shock and that surprise, where shall I get now?

Har lahza tazaa tazaa balaaon ka saamna
Naa aazmooda kaar ki jur'at kahaan se laaein

Hai aaj bhi nigaah-e muhabbat ki aarzu
Per aisi ik nigaah ki qeemat kahaan se laaein

Sab kuchh naseeb ho bhi to ai shorish-e hayaat
Tujh se nazar churaane ki aadat kahaan se laaein

A new disaster, each passing moment, each day
But the courage of a novice, where shall I get now?

I crave for a glance of love even now, my love!
The cost for such a glance, where shall I get now?

My life's upheavals! What if I have my wish granted?
The nerve to evade your looks, where shall I get now?

28

Jan Nisar Akhtar

Jan Nisar Akhtar (1914–1976), son of the famous Urdu poet Muztar Khairabadi, hailed from a family of eminent poets and men of letters. He was born in Gwalior, where he received his early education before joining Aligarh Muslim University. He began his career as an academic who taught at Victoria College, Gwalior, then at Hamidia College, Bhopal. He was closely associated with the Progressive Writers Movement of which he also became the president. Later, he shifted to Bombay and joined the film industry as a lyricist and wrote some of the most haunting lyrics.

Akhtar started writing in the romantic tradition, but later subscribed to Progressive aesthetics which had become the model of the day. He developed an individual signature, clearly distinguishable from his contemporaries. He disengaged himself from the aesthetics which had become the model of the day, and from the Progressive writers, who treated literature as a site for slogan-raising and propaganda. Akhtar's poetry is a fine example where message is artfully rendered in a lyrical mode. His poetry collections include *Nazr-e Butaan, Salaasil, Pichhla Peher, Ghar Aangan, Khaak-e Dil, Taar-e Garebaan* and *Jaavedaan.* The letters that his wife, Safia Akhtar, had written to him were put together in *Zer-e Lub* and *Harf Aashnaa.* They were later collected in *Tumhare Naam.* The letters unravel the tales of their lives lived with remarkable sincerity, and a deeper understanding of their severe limitations.

I

Fursat-e kaar faqat chaar ghadi hai yaaro
Ye na socho ke abhi umr padi hai yaaro

Apne taareek makaanon se to baahar niklo
Zindgai shama liye dar pe khadi hai yaaro

Hum ne sadiyon inhi zarron se muhabbat kee hai
Sub'ha aaee hai magar door khadi hai yaaro

Kis ki dehleez pe le jaa ke sajaaein us ko
Beech raste mein koee laash padi hai yaaro

Un ke bin jee ke dikhaa denge unhein yoon hi sahi
Baat itni hai ke zid aan padi hai yaaro

I

Just a few moments for the deed, O my friends
Don't say life is long to succeed, O my friends

Emerge from your dark cloisters, reach up for the door
Life waits with a guiding lamp to lead, O my friends

I have loved these specks for millions of years
The dawn has shown but shies indeed, O my friends

Whose door do I choose, which one do I embellish?
A corpse on the road is lying to proceed, O my friends

I will live without her; I will show how I can
Now let that be my only creed, O my friends

2

Ash'aar mere yoon to zamaane ke liye hain
Kuchh sher faqat un ko sunaane ke liye hain

Ye bhi to naheen theek ke har dard mitaa dein
Kuchh dard kaleje se lagaane ke liye hain

Aankhon mein jo bhar loge to kante se chubhenge
Ye khwaab to palkon pe sajaane ke liye hain

Dekhoon tere hathon ko to lagtaa hai tere haath
Mandir mein faqat deep jalaane ke liye hain

Socho to badi cheez hai tehzeeb badan ki
Warna to badan aag bujhaane ke liye hain

Ye 'ilm ka sauda, ye risaale, ye kitaabein
Ek shakhsh ki yaadon ko bhulaane ke liye hain

2

My verses are for the world to cheer
But only a few lines for you to hear

But how can I erase all my pains?
May I have some pains to hold them dear?

If you hold them close, they will prick your eyes
They are dreams for the eyelashes to cheer

When I look at your hands, I find your hands
Are made to put the temple lamps in cheer

This body's piety is a boon I know
It's also to quench its raging fire here

All this living among books and journals
Is only to keep her memories in clear

29

Majrooh Sultanpuri

Majrooh Sultanpuri (1919–2000) is the nom de plume of Asrarul Hasan Khan. He was born in village Nizamabad of qasba Azamgarh. He received his education on the pattern of *Dars-e Nizami* with an emphasis on Arabic, Persian and religious knowledge. Later, he earned a degree in traditional Unani medicine from Lucknow, which he practised but relinquished soon. Majrooh joined the Bombay film industry as a lyricist and wrote many memorable songs. He won Filmfare's Best Lyricist Award and then the most prestigious Dada Sahib Phalke Lifetime Achievement Award. He subscribed to the aesthetics of Progressive Writers Movement, staunchly believed in Marxist philosophy, was imprisoned for his leftist leanings, but was finally disenchanted with the way socialism had chosen to follow of late in Russia and China.

Majrooh earned his reputation essentially as a poet of the classical ghazal tradition. He knew the standards of the traditional poetics well enough to be able to use it to his benefit and acquire an individual voice in the melee of voices around. Majrooh allowed his ghazal to remain a traditional ghazal in its essential make-up, even though he found ways to insert contemporary realities into its content and form, following the norms of the modern poetics. He published his poetry in *Ghazal* and *Mis'hal-e Jaan*.

I

Hum hain mat'aa-e kucha-o bazaar ki tarah
Uthh'ti hai har nigaah khareedaar ki tarah

Wo to kaheen hain aur magar dil ke aas paas
Phirti hai koee shai nigah-e yaar ki tarah

Is kue tashnagi main bahut hai ke ek Jaam
Haath aa gayaa hai daulat-e bedaar ki tarah

Seedhi hai raah-e shauq pa yoon hi kaheen kaheen
Khum ho gaee hai gesu-i- dildaar ki tarah

Be tesha-i nazar na chalo raah-e raftagaan
Har naqsh-e paa baland hai deewaar ki tarah

Ab jaa ke kuchh khula hunar-e naakhun-e junoon
Zakhnm-e jigar hue lab-o rukhsaar ki tarah

Majrooh likh rahe hain wo ahl-e wafaa ke naam
Hum bhee khade hue hain gunahgaar ki tarah

I

Each buyer surveys the wares in the market
And I—like only a ware in the market

She is not here, but close to my heart, here
Something lurks about—like her fleeting glance

In the home of thirst, a cup of drink is luck
Like a treat of fate—like a gift in hand

The way to the cherished goal is laid straight
Coiled but here and there—like her curly tresses

Don't walk the older paths without much caution
Each footprint is amazing—like the high walls

Only now I can guess what artful nails can do
The wounds of heart have become—like lips and cheeks

Majrooh! He's scribbling the names of lovers
I too stand with them—like a damned sinner

2

Hum ko junoon kya sikhlaate ho, hum the pareshaan
tum se ziyaada
Phaade honge hum ne azizo, chaak garebaan tum se ziyaada

Chaak-e jigar muhtaaj-e rafoo hai aaj to daaman sirf luhoo hai
Ek mausam tha hum ko raha hai shauq-e bahaaraan
tum se ziyaada

'Ahd-e wafa yaaron se nibhaaein, naz-e harifaan hans ke uthhaaein
Jab ye armaan tum se siwaa tha, ab hain pashemaan
tum se ziyaada

Hum bhi hameshaa qatl hue aur tum ne bhi dekha door se lekin
Ye na samajhna hum ko hua hai, jaan ka nuqsaan
tum se ziyaada

Jaao tum apne baam ki khaatir, saari lawein shammon ki katar lo
Zakhm ke mehr-o maah salaamat, jashn-e chiraaghaan
tum se ziyaada

Dekh ke uljhan zulf-e dota ki kaise ulajh padte hain hawaa se
Hum se seekho hum ko hai yaaro fikr-e nigaaraan tum se ziyaada

Zanjeer-o deewar hi dekhi tum ne to Majrooh magar hum
Koocha koocha dekh rahe hain aalam-e zindaan tum se ziyaada

2

Don't tell me what being crazy is; I was the one,
and more than you
I must have torn my own clothes many a time,
and more than you

The torn heart calls for relief for I stand smeared in blood
But there was a time I cherished the spring, and
more than you

Let me keep my words with friends, suffer the follies of my foes
My desires soared high but now I'm humbled,
and more than you

You kept apart, you watched me slay, every time I met my fate
Don't think I've suffered more but I've surely pined,
and more than you

Go and prune the wicks of lamps to light your homes, both in and out
Let my wounds live for long, I shall have the lights,
and more than you

Looking at those curls of tresses, how you curse the
ruffling wind
Look at me, learn from me, how I cared for her,
and more than you

You have only seen the four walls and the iron chains, Majrooh
But I've seen prison houses in every street, and more than you

NEW POETICS

The mid-twentieth century saw the emergence of what may be called the new ghazal. It was new as poetry elsewhere and in other languages too was new. While some poets from India and the newly-created Pakistan drew upon past traditions to develop their own models of the decisively modern, others broke completely free from them to project their novel, drastic or even desperate versions of what can, in retrospect, be ambivalently called the postmodern. This liberal stance towards life and art resulted in the emergence of a large variety of thematic and stylistic variations. Exposed to contemporary realities of the time, the new poets wrote of existential angst, turned the abstract into concrete and the concrete into abstract, the mundane into sublime and the sublime into mundane.

The new generation of poets lived in an increasingly shrinking world of migrations and diasporas, even while inhabiting an expanding world of doubt and faith, belonging and estrangement. Experimenting with language—resorting to intermixing of various linguistic codes, turning playful with it to evolve a secular parlance—turned out be their credo. Some of them even went to the extent of writing the 'anti-ghazal' by defying the age-old principles of poetics. They aimed at evolving a unique diction, with a fresh usage of metaphors and moods, images and moments, channelling auditory and visual elements in these. In moulding the contemporary speech as gendered, communal, political or even prosaic, they wished to manoeuvre their compositions in their individual style. Thereby, the new poets also experimented with form, breaking the traditional moulds of the ghazal. They showed immense intellectual curiosity and carried it closer to other arts. They turned to the avant-garde and the surrealist modes of poetry, chose to be allusive and ambiguous, as well as downright playful and humourous. At the same time, they also turned mythopoeic in their perceptions of the historical and literary time.

As the new poets represented their times and climes, they also tested themselves in a larger melting pot of the native and non-native cultures. They constituted a part of the socio-political condition of their times defined by some of the major events in south Asian history, like the lingering shadows of India's Partition (1947), the Indo–China war (1962), India–Pakistan wars (1965, 1971, 1999), India's nuclear experiments (1974, 1998), and the unending skirmishes between peoples and nations. The new poets found their ways of assent and dissent in the way they internalized the conditions around them in the spirit of curiosity, interrogation, escape and affirmation.

30

Majeed Amjad

Majeed Amjad (1914–1974), who lived a very private life and had little respect for extra-literary considerations, was born in Jhung (now in Pakistan). He received his early education in Arabic and Persian at a local mosque, and continued his education there before going to Islamia College, Lahore, to get his bachelor's degree. He began his career as a journalist, editing the weekly *Urooj*, which was published from Jhung. It was there that he started publishing his poetry, and was later fired from his job for publishing a poem against the British Raj. Amjad joined the Civil Supplies Department and kept moving from place to place.

Amjad is a typical case of an acknowledged but ignored genius. Although in serious critical appraisals he has been rated as one of the most remarkable poets to determine the contours of modern Urdu poetry, he continues to be read less and evaluated even lesser. His poetry is a configuration of memory, metaphor and space. What distinguishes all these configurations is his narrative, which has the ability to carry the reader forward in time and space. He is a poet of the nazm, but his ghazals shake hands with the techniques he employed in his nazm, with respect to the constructions of myths and metaphors, language and modes of narration. *Shab-e Rafta* is the only collection he published during his lifetime; *Mere Khuda Mere Dil* and his collected works, *Kulliyaat-e Majeed Amjad,* were published posthumously.

I

Jung bhee, tera dhyaan bhee, hum bhee
Siren bhee, azaaan bhee, hum bhee

Sab teri hi amaan mein shab bedaar
Morche bhee, makaan bhee, hum bhee

Teri manshaaon ke mahaaz pe hain
Chhaauni ke jawaan bhee, hum bhee

Dekhne wale ye nazaara bhi dekh
'Azm bhee, imtihaan bhee, hum bhee

Ek ajab etamaad seenon mein
Fat'ha ka ye nishaan bhee, hum bhee

Too bhee aur teri nafraton ke saath
Shahr mein Tikka Khan bhee, hum bhee

I

The war, your nagging thoughts, and me too
That siren, this call for prayer, and me too

All of them in your care, all night long
Those frontiers, these abodes, and me too

They are on the borders of your target
Those soldiers from the cantonment, and me too

Onlooker! Come and look at this scene too
This resolve and this trial, and me too

There is a strange confidence in hearts
This very sign of victory, and me too

You, and with all your hatred, all over
That is Tikka Khan in town, and me too

2

Her waqt fikr-e-marg-e ghareebaana chaahiye
Sáihat ka ek pehloo mareezaana chaahiye

Dunya-i be-tareeq mein jis samt bhi chalo
Raste mein ek salaam rafeeqaana chaahiye

Aankhon mein umde rooh ki nazdeekiyon ke saath
Aisa bhi ek door ka yaarana chaahiye

Kya pastiyon ki zillatein kya azmaton ke fauz
Apne liye 'azaab judaagaana chaahiye

Ab dard-e-shash bhi saans ki koshish mein hai shareek
Ab kya ho, ab to neend ko aa jaana chaahiye

Raushan taraaiyon se utarti hawa mein aaj
Do char gaam laghzish-e mastaana chaahiye

Amjad un ashk bar zamaanon ke waaste
Ek saa'at-e-bahaar ka nazraana chaahiye

2

Only to die a humble death is all I desire
Ailment as a face of health is all I desire

Whichever way I move in a rowdy world, I may
Only a kind greeting on the way is all I desire

May all the warmth of souls light up bright in the eyes
Such a distant bond of souls is all I desire

What humiliation in pits! What glory in heights!
A different curse for myself is all I desire

Now the abundance of pain joins the efforts of breaths
What now, now the sleep's arrival is all I desire!

With the winds descending from the luminous foothills
To walk a few wobbling steps is all I desire

Amjad! What do I want for those tearful days?
Only a moment's spring of joy is all I desire

3I

Ada Jafarey

Ada Jafarey (1924–2015) is the nom de plume of Aziz Jahan, the first woman poet from Pakistan, who was widely read and recognized. She received six prestigious awards from literary organizations and the government of Pakistan. She was born in Badayun in Uttar Pradesh, India, to a family of traditional values. The sheer need to express herself took her spontaneously to writing poetry. This turned out to be a way of finding an individual voice and making a permanent place for herself in the emerging literary circles of Pakistan.

Jafarey blended the personal and the social, and created a complex dynamics that negotiated the self with the other. Being essentially romantic in its make-up, her poetry is sensitive in its apprehension of internal and external realities. Her first collection, *Main Saaz Dhoondti Rahi*, was followed by *Shahr-e*

Dard, Ghazalaan Tum to Waaqif Ho, Saaz-e Sukhan Bahaana Hai, Harf-e Shanaasaayi, Safar Baaqi Hai and *Mausam Mausam.*

I

Hoton pe kabhi un ke tera naam hi aai
Aai to sahi barsar-e ilzaam hi aai

Hairaan hain, lab basta hain, dilgeer hain ghunche
Khushbu ki zabaani tera paighaam hi aai

Lamhaat-e musarrat hain tassawur se gurezaan
Yaad aai hain jab bhi gham-o aalaam hi aai

Kya raah badalne ka gila humsafaron se
Jis rah se chale tere dar-o baam hi aai

Thak haar ke baithhe hain sar-e koo-e tamanna
Kaam aai to phir jazba-i naakaam hi aai

Baaqi na rahe saakh Ada dasht-e junoon ki
Dil mein agar andesha-i anjaam hi aai

I

Let your name touch her lips, let that happen
Let that be yet for a blame, let that happen

Blossoms wonder; they are sad and silent too
May the fragrance bring your word, let that happen

The moments of pleasure are shy of my thoughts
Let me recall pains and pangs, let that happen

Why grudge the fellow travellers the change of path?
The path I choose may reach you, let that happen

I'm tired; I sit forlorn by the lane of desire
Let the failed emotions matter, let that happen

This wilderness, Ada, will surely prove worth its name
Let the fear of end crop in mind, let that happen

2

Na ghubaar mein na gulaab mein mujhe dekhnaa
Mere dard ke tab-o taab mein mujhe dekhnaa

Kisee waqt shaam-e malaal mein mujhe sochnaa
Kabhi apne dil ki kitaab mein mujhe dekhnaa

Kisee raat maah-o nujoom se mujhe poochhna
Kabhi apni chashm-e pur aab mein mujhe dekhnaa

Main na mil sakoon bhi to kya hua ke fasaana hoon
Nayi daastaan naye baab mein mujhe dekhnaa

Main jo raat bhar gham-e aftaab-e sehar mein thee
Usee shola roo ke 'ataab mein mujhe dekhnaa

Isee dil se ho ke guzar gaye kaee karwaan
Kaee hijraton ke nesaab mein mujhe dekhnaa

Mere khaar khaar sawaal mein mujhe dhoondnaa
Mere geet mein mere khwaab mein mujhe dekhnaa

Mere aansuon ne bujhaaee thee meri tashnagi
Usi barguzeeda shabaab mein mujhe dekhnaa

Wahi ek lamha-i deed tha ke ruka rahaa
Mere roz-o shab ke hisaab mein mujhe dekhnaa

Jo tadap tujhe kisee aaeene mein na mil sake
To phir aaeene ke jawaab mein mujhe dekhnaa

2

Not in dust, not in roses, look for me
Only in my glowing pains, look for me

Think of me in a sad and gloomy dusk
Someday, in my heart's tome, look for me

Ask the moon, the stars for me one night
Someday, in your tearful eyes, look for me

A lost story, what if I am not found
In a new tale, a new part, look for me

All night I mourned the morning sun's demise
In the rage of its blazing face, look for me

Many caravans crossed this heart's horizon
In the course of those migrations, look for me

Look for me in all my thorny questions
In my songs, in my dreams, look for me

My tears alone had slaked my thirst one day
In my own glorious youth, look for me

That moment froze in time, when I saw you
In my nights' and days' accounts, look for me

If you can't see the pain's throb in mirror
Then in the mirror's reply, look for me

32

Nasir Kazmi

Nasir Kazmi (1925–1972), born Syed Nasir Raza Kazmi in Ambala, Punjab, is one of the most celebrated poets of Pakistan. As he moved from place to place, he received his education in different places like Ambala, Peshawar, Simla and Lahore. In his professional life, he worked as a staff editor with Radio Pakistan, a journalist with *Auraq-e Nau* and as the editor-in-chief of *Humayoon*.

Kazmi began writing ghazals in a typical romantic mode. However, he soon matured into a poet who could contest stereotypical romanticism by developing a complex dialogue with the self and the natural elements, and by speaking in a language that was both personal and impersonal. Poetry, for him, became a way of transforming the perishable into imperishable, and the imperishable into immortal, by turns.

Nature, fine arts and finer human emotions emerged as language personified in his *shers*, as he moved from one condition of being to another. This master of metaphors and the short-metre *shers* has four collections to his credit: *Barg-e Nai*, *Deewan*, *Pehli Baarish* and *Nishaat-e Khwaab*, apart from a poetic play, *Sur ki Chchaayaa*, an anthology of miscellaneous prose writings titled *Khushk Chashme ke Kinaare* and a diary titled *Nasir Kazmi ki Diary*. He also edited and compiled selections from the master poets like Vali Deccani, Mir Taqi Mir, Syed Inshaallah Khan Insha and Nazeer Akbarabadi.

I

Rahnaward-e bayaabaan-e gham, sabr kar sabr kar
Kaarwaan phir milenge baham, sabr kar sabr kar

Benishaan hai safar, raat saari padi hai magar
Aa rahi hai sadaa dum ba dum, sabr kar sabr kar

Teri faryaad goonjegi dharti se aakaash tak
Koee din aur sah le sitam, sabr kar sabr kar

Shahr ujde to kya, hai kushaada zameen-e Khuda
Ek naya ghar banaaenge hum, sabr kar sabr kar

Bastiyon mein andhera sahi, ghum ka dera sahi
Phir naee sub'ha legi janam, sabr kar sabr kar

Ye mahallat-e shaahi tabaahi ke hain muntazir
Girne waale hain un ke 'alam, sabr kar sabr kar

Lehlahaaengi phir khetiyaan, kaarwaan kaarwaan
Khul ke barsega abr-e karam, sabr kar sabr kar

Duf bajaaenge barg-o-shajar, saf-ba-saf, har taraf
Khushk mitti se phootegaa num, sabr kar sabr kar

I

Passers-by in pain's wilderness; have patience, a little patience
The caravans will join again; have patience, a little patience

The long journey knows no aim; the lingering night
knows no end
I hear a voice time and again; have patience, a little patience

Your imploring will resound from the earth to skies afar
Bear the pain a few days again; have patience, a little patience

What if the towns are ravaged, my God's country is so immense?
We shall build our abodes again; have patience, a little patience

No matter if hamlets gloomy, no worry if worries swarm
We shall surely meet at dawn; have patience, a little patience

The royal palaces will thrive for sure till they perish one day
The crowns will surely fall apart; have patience, a little patience

All the farms would bear fruit; caravans too would make a move
Again, the clouds will bring the rains; have patience, a little
patience

Fruits and foliage shall play the drums in rows, all around
Arid soil shall be moist again; have patience, a little patience

Kyun pataktaa hai sar sung se, jee jalaa dhang se
Dil hi bun jaaega khud sanam, sabr kar sabr kar

Pahle khil jaai dil ka kanwal, phir likhenge ghazal
Koee dum ai sareer-e qalam, sabr kar sabr kar

Dard ke taar milne to de, hont hilne to de
Saari baatein karenge raqam, sabr kar sabr kar

Dekh Nasir zamaane mein koee kisee ka naheen
Bhool ja us ke qaul-o qasam, sabr kar sabr kar

Why beat your head against the rock, why burn in pain,
why suffer?
The hearts will themselves bear love; have patience,
a little patience

Let the heart's lotus bloom first, I will write my verse later
Wait a while my pen's lyre; have patience, a little patience

Let the tunes of pain come together, let the lips shake too
We shall pen them all together; have patience, a little patience

Look here, Nasir, no one cares for anyone in this selfish
world
You must forget all those vows and have patience,
a little patience

2

Apni dhun mein rehta hoon
Main bhee tere jaisa hoon

O pichhli rut ke saathi
Ab ke baras main tanha hoon

Teri gali mein saaraa din
Dukh ke kankar chunta hoon

Mujh se aankh milaai kaun
Main tera aaeena hoon

Mera diya jalaai kaun
Main tera khaali kamra hoon

Tu jeewan ki bhari gali
Main jungle ka rasta hoon

Apni lehar hai apna rog
Darya hoon aur pyasa hoon

Aati rut mujhe roegi
Jaati rut ka jhonka hoon

2

I too am lost to myself
I too am only like you

O my friend of last season!
This season I am in blue

All day long in your lane
Pain's pebbles I pick anew

Who can see me in my eyes?
I am but your image true

Who would light my silent lamp?
I'm your empty rendezvous

You, a busy lane of life
Me, a path in jungle's queue

It's my pleasure, it's my pain
I'm a brook but thirsty too

The next spring shall mourn me
A dying dirge of season's blue!

33

Ibn-e Insha

Ibn-e Insha (1927–1978) is the nom de plume of Sher Mohammad Khan who was born in Phillaur tehsil of Jalandhar district in the Punjab of British India. He received his BA from Punjab University and MA from the University of Karachi. He worked in various capacities in the government that included positions at Radio Pakistan, the Ministry of Culture and the National Book Centre of Pakistan. His stint at the United Nations provided him with an opportunity to travel throughout the world and write his inimitable travelogues.

A poet, humourist, travelogue writer and columnist, Insha wrote like none else before him, nor did anyone after him. The most remarkable features of his poetry and prose lay in his use of language and the tone and tenor that he employed to represent a mood, a situation or a condition. He is direct in his address, intimate in his tone, witty in apprehension and completely unassuming in approach. He evolved a language for his purpose with a mix of Urdu and Hindi, and created a narrative of intimacy. His collections of poems are *Is Basti ke Ek Kooche Mein*, *Chaand Nagar* and *Dil-e Wahshi*. He also wrote five travelogues and four books of humorous writing.

I

Kuchh kahne ka waqt naheen ye kuchh na kaho khaamosh raho
Ai logo khaamosh raho haan ai logo khaamosh raho

Such achha per us ki jadon mein zehr ka hai ek pyala bhi
Paagal ho kyun naahaq ko Suqraat bano khaamosh raho

Haq achha per us ke liye koee aur mare to aur achha
Tum bhi koee Mansoor ho jo sooli pe chadho khaamosh raho

Un ka ye kehna sooraj hi dharti ke phere kartaa hai
Sar aankhon sooraj hi ko ghoomne do khaamosh raho

Majlis mein kuchh habs hai aur zanjeer ka aahan chubhta hai
Phir socho haan phir socho haan phir socho khaamosh raho

Garm aansoon aur thandi aanhein man mein kya kya mausam
hain
Is bagiya ke bhed na kholo, sair karo, khaamosh raho

Aankhein moond kinaare baithhoon mun ke rakhhoon bund
kiwaad
Insha ji lo dhaaga lo aur lub see lo khaamosh raho

I

Not the time to speak up, don't speak, just keep shut
Keep shut my friends, yes, my friends, just keep shut

Truth is fine but their roots keep a poison bowl too
Are you mad? Are you Socrates? Just keep shut

Truth is virtue but let someone else die for truth
Are you Mansoor? Why at the altar? Just keep shut

He says it's the sun that keeps moving around the earth
Accept all that, let the sun move, just keep shut

It's suffocating all around, the iron chains pinch too
Think again, then think again, yes think again, just keep shut

Hot tears and cold sighs—strange seasons my heart has
known
Don't reveal the garden's secret, just keep walking, just keep
shut

Let me shut my eyes, sit aside, keep the doors of heart closed
Insha-ji! Here's the thread, just sew up your lips, just keep
shut

2

Kaisi bhi ho us shakhs ki auqaat azizo
Insha ki ghaneemat hai abhi zaat azizo

Is shahr-e khirad mein kahaan milte hain diwane
Paida to karo us se mulaaqaat azizo

Paaband-e-salaasil hai pa zindaan-e-jahaan mein
Rindaan-e-jahaan ki see kare baat azizo

Hai muflis-o muhtaaj pa hum ne to na dekha
Us ko ba dar-e qibala-i haajaat azizo

Paaya hai magar khaak basar ahl-e talab mein
Utri ho jahaan husn ki baaraat azizo

Is shakhs ne yoon kaun saa maidaan naheen maara
Bas ishq ki baazi mein hui maat azizo

Us mein bhi rahaa haath ye sheeraaza sukhan ka
Usshaq ke matlab ki ghazaleeyaat azizo

2

Whatever be the rank of that being, my dear friends
Insha is even now a precious being, my dear friends

A frenzied one in the city of the wise! No chance
Go and make friends with that very being, my dear friends

He is in chains but in this world's prison house
He talks just like the drunken ones, my dear friends

He's poor, he's needy, but I haven't seen him ever
At the door of the obliging Lords, my dear friends

I've found him on the ground in the seekers' company
Where the beauteous beings descend, my dear friends

Has he left a space unconquered; he hasn't indeed
He lost only on the love's ground, my dear friends

Even there, he had his hand in rolling out verses
Such verses that appealed to lovers, my dear friends

34

Khalilur Rehman Azmi

Khalilur Rehman Azmi (1927–1978) was born in village Seda Sultanpur in the district of Azamgarh, India. He received his early education in Azamgarh before he joined Aligarh Muslim University to acquire higher degrees. He ultimately became an Urdu faculty in the university, and came to distinguish himself as a poet and critic who underlined the contours of modernism in Urdu literature.

As an academic and an acknowledged critic of the Progressive Writers Movement, Azmi had the unique advantage of defining his own role as a poet. He began writing poetry, like many others, under the impact of romanticism, but matured into someone who could think of the evolution of metaphor in his poetry, and assess the new poetics in relation to his own practice. Perceptions of time and ironic overtones in expression distinguished his poetry in his collections, *Naya*

'Ahd Naamah, Kaaghazi Pairahan and *Zindagi Ay Zindagi*. Selections from these collections were later put together in *Aasman Ay Aasman*. He also published a critical work on the Progressive Writers Movement, apart from editing the first comprehensive anthology of modern Urdu poetry entitled *Naee Nazm Ka Safar* with another well-known poet and colleague, Munibur Rehman.

I

Wo rang-e rukh wo aatish-e khoon kaun le gaya
Ai dil tera wo raqs-e junoon kaun le gaya

Zanjir aansuon ki kahaan toot kar giri
Wo intihaa-i gham ka sukoon kaun le gaya

Dard-e nihaan ke chheen liye kis ne aaeene
Nok-e mizha se qatra-i khoon kaun le gaya

Jo mujh se bolti theen wo raatein kahaan gaeen
Jo jaagta tha soz-e duroon kaun le gaya

Kis mode pe bichhad gaye khwabon ke qaafile
Wo manzil-e tarab ka fusoon kaun le gaya

Jo shama itni raat jali kyun wo bujh gaee
Jo shauq ho chalaa tha fuzoon kaun le gaya

I

That glamour, that gurgle of blood—who took them all away?
Who robbed the heart of the wild dance—who took
them all away?

Where did the chains of tears break, where did they
break at last?
Where are my tranquil sorrows—who took them all away?

Who robbed me of the mirror that showed me my
hidden pains?
Those drops of blood from eyelashes—who took
them all away?

Where have the nights gone, the nights that spoke to me once?
The silent ache that kept throbbing—who took them all away?

At what turn the caravan of dreams lost their track with me?
The magic of the blissful goal—who took them all away?

Why did the lamp go to sleep, the lamp that burnt all night?
The desires that soared high—who took them all away?

2

Main kahaan hoon kuchh bata de zindagi ai zindagi
Phir sadaa apni suna de zindagi ai zindagi

So gaye ek ek kar ke khaana-i dil ke chiraagh
Un chiraagon ko jaga de zindagi ai zindagi

Wo bisaat-e sher-o naghma, rat-jage, wo chahchahe
Phir wahi mehfil saja de zindagi ai zindagi

Jis ke har qatre se rug rug mein machalta tha lahu
Phir wahi ek shai pila de zindagi ai zindagi

Ab to yaad aataa naheen kaisaa tha apnaa rang roop
Phir meri surat dikha de zindagi ai zindagi

Ek muddat ho gaee roothha hoon apne aap se
Phir mujhe mujh se mila de zindagi ai zindagi

Jaane bargashta hai kyun mujh se zamaane ki hawa
Apne daaman ki hawa de zindagi ai zindagi

Ruch gaya hai meri nus nus mein meri raaton ka zahr
Mere sooraj ko bula de zindagi ai zindagi

2

Where do I linger, tell me, O life, my life
Let me hear your songs again, O life, my life

One by one, all the lamps of the heart went to sleep
Wake them up once again, O life, my life

The sallies of words, lively nights, that hubbub
Let them come alive again, O life, my life

The drop that made the blood gurgle in my veins
Let me drink that drop again, O life, my life

I don't remember what my look, what my mien
Show me now my face again, O life, my life

It's ages now, I've been sulking with myself
Let me now meet myself, O life, my life

Why is the world cross with me, I don't know why!
Be kind to me, be kind again, O life, my life

Night's poison has gone deep, deep into my veins
Now call my sun, call it now, O life, my life

35

Hasan Naim

Hasan Naim (1927–1991), named Syed Hasan and mentioned in the family tree as Syed Shah Hasan Naim after his father, was born in Patna to a family which had major Sufi saints as ancestors. He received his school and early college education in Patna. Later, he went to Aligarh Muslim University for his bachelor's degree in science, and there, he also got an opportunity to prune his literary taste. Beginning his professional career as a schoolteacher in Patna and Calcutta, he went on to join the Ministry of External Affairs in Delhi. A series of assignments outside India gave him the opportunity to enrich his poetic taste. After completing his foreign assignments, he worked as the director of the All India Ghalib Centenary Committee, which led to the establishment of the Ghalib Institute (Aiwan-e Ghalib) in Delhi, an institution he served with great dedication, but not without controversy. Naim spent the rest of his days in disease, despair, silence and penury.

Although Naim aligned himself with the Progressive Writers Association ideologically, he disapproved of their poetics and sought a mode of expression that could sustain new consciousness. An abundance of ideas and thoughts characterized his poetry. These ideas oscillated between doubt and faith, and the secular and the spiritual. His poetic strategy lay in executing multiple allusions and in exploiting the ambiguities of language. He was fully aware of the demands that the new ghazal made and he met them with critical discretion. Naim has left behind three collections of his poems—*Ash'aar*, *Ghazalnaama* (in Hindi) and *Dabistaan*.

I

Karein na yaad shab-e haadasa hua so hua
Bhula dein aao her ek waaqeya hua so hua

Bura hua ke lade jaan nisaar aapas mein
Bura hai aur bhi ye tazkira hua so hua

Ghazab hua ke naye log aa base dil mein
Bichhadna un se alag saaneha hua so hua

Kahaan kahaan se na aafat ki badliyaan aaeein
Dayaar-e qalb mein jo zalzala hua so hua

Bahut se kante gire phool ban ke daaman per
Gulon ki zaat se jo faaida hua so hua

Pehen ke dost bhi nikle libaas-e tanz Hasan
Wo apni aan mein beqaaida hua so hua

I

Let's forget that terrible night, whatever happened, happened
Let's forget that dreadful sight, whatever happened,
happened

It was really sad the lovers picked a deadly brawl
Talking about a bigger blight, whatever happened, happened

Awful! Some new faces found their homes in hearts
Parting but was a sad plight, whatever happened, happened

Dark clouds gathered around, spelling calamity
Hearts got a terrible fright, whatever happened, happened

Many a thorn fell like blossoms into my cozy lap
Blossoms brought such delight, whatever happened,
happened

Even friends with their sarcasm, Hasan, found their way
ahead
They were though full of spite, whatever happened, happened

2

Husn ki sehr-o karaamaat se jee darta hai
Ishq ki zinda riwaayaat se jee darta hai

Main ne maana ke mujhe un se mohabbat na rahi
Hamnaheen phir bhi mulaaqaat se jee darta hai

Such to ye hai ke abhi dil ko sukoon hai lekin
Apne aawaaraa khayaalaat se jee darta hai

Itna roya hoon gham-e dost zara saa hans kar
Muskuraai hue lamhaat se jee darta hai

Kis ghadi kaun si wahshat mein kare mujh ko shareek
Ishq ki ek isee baat se jee darta hai

Jo bhi kehna ho kaho saaf shikaayat hi sahi
In ishiraat-o kinaayaat se jee darta hai

Hijr ka dard naee baat naheen hai lekin
Din wo guzra hai ke ab raat se jee darta hai

Kaun bhoola hai Naim un ki mohabbat ka fareb
Phir bhi un taaza inaayaat se jee darta hai

2

I'm scared of love's kindness, I'm scared
I'm scared of love's eternal ways, I'm scared

I know I don't love her now anymore, I don't
I'm scared of meeting her again, I'm scared

True, I'm at rest; my heart is also calm now
I'm scared of my roving thoughts, I'm scared

Love's sorrow! I've wept so much, after a smile
I'm scared of the smiling moments, I'm scared

Who knows what wild acts it may get me in, and when
I'm scared of this very way of love, I'm scared

Say what you have to say, even make a complaint
I'm scared of these and those signs, I'm scared

The pain of parting is nothing new, even then
I'm scared of the night, as of the day, I'm scared

I haven't forgotten, Naim, the illusions lived in love
I'm scared of the new compassions, I'm scared

36

Mohammad Alvi

Mohammad Alvi (1927–2018) was born in Ahmedabad, Gujarat, where he lived all his life. A man of little formal education, Alvi hailed from the business community of his home-town.

Alvi can be called a typical avant-garde Urdu poet, who broke all the established traditions of the classical and the Progressive poets in the way he excercised his poetic diction, and used images, metaphors and symbols. He evolved his own methods of turning a bizarre idea into a poem. Alvi strengthened this poetic method further by appropriating a diction that is now childlike, now monologist, and now too prosaic to be even seemingly poetic. He was a rebel without proclaiming to be one. He made his mark with his very first collection of poems, *Khaali Makaan*, which was followed by *Aakhiri Din Ki Talaash*, *Teesri Kitaab* and *Chauthaa Aasman*, which won him the Sahitya Akademi Award and also an award from the Gujarat Urdu Academy.

I

Ghar ne apna hosh sambhaala din nikla
Khidki mein bhar gaya ujaala din nikla

Laal gulabi hua ufuq ka darwaaza
Toot gaya sooraj ka taala din nikla

Pedon per chup rahne waali raat gaee
Shaakh shaakh pe bolne waala din nikla

Naye naye manzar aankhon mein phail gaye
Khula koee rangeen risaala din nikla

Aankhein kholo, khwab sameto, jaago bhi
Alvi pyare dekho saala din nikla

I

To its senses came the abode, appeared the day
Then the sleeping windows glowed, appeared the day

Red and pink turned the threshold of the horizon
Breaking its lock, the sun showed, appeared the day

Perching silent on the trees the night met its end
The swinging boughs the birds rode, appeared the day

New landscapes showed up bright before the eyes
A lively site then bestowed, appeared the day

Open your eyes, fold your dreams, wake up now
Alvi dear, break your mode, appeared the day

2

Roshni kuchh to mile jungle mein
Aag lag jaai ghane jungle mein

Aap ko shahr mein dar lagta hai
Hum to bekhauf rahe jungle mein

Ek ek shaakh zaban ho jaai
Koee aawaaz to de jungle mein

Ped se ped lagaa rehtaa hai
Pyar hota hai ghane jungle mein

Shahr mein kaan taraste hi rahe
Chahchahe hum ne sune jungle mein

Shaam hote hi utar aate hain
Shokh pariyon ke pare jungle mein

Shokh hirnon ne qalaanchein maareen
More ke raqs hue jungle mein

Ab bhi qadmon ke nishaan milte hain
Gaaon se door pare jungle mein

Ab bhi phirti hai koee parchchaaeen
Raat ke waqt bhare jungle mein

Khoob the hazrat-e Adam Alvi
Bastiyaan chhod gaye jungle mein

2

Let there be some light in the jungle
Let some fire ignite in the jungle

You stay scared in the city
I lived with no fright in the jungle

Let each bough speak as a tongue
Let a call alight in the jungle

The trees stand embracing trees
Love glows so bright in the jungle

Ears craved for a tweet in the city
Birds chirped with delight in the jungle

They all descend when the evening does
A flock of meteorites in the jungle

Naughty deer, all jump in joy
Peacock's dance excited in the jungle

Even now, footprints appear
Far from village, bright in the jungle

Even now, there moves a shadow
During a dark night in the jungle

Adam was so wise, Alvi
He kept the sylvan site in the jungle

37

Munir Niazi

Munir Niazi (1928–2006) was born in a village called Khanpur, near Hoshiarpur in Punjab, India. After the 1947 Partition, he migrated to Pakistan and settled in Sahiwal, where he completed his school education. Later, he went to Bahawalpur and Lahore for his college education. He launched a journal called *Saat Rang*, wrote lyrics for films, established a publishing institute called *Al-Misaal* and wrote for radio and newspapers as a freelancer. He also worked for the Pakistan Television Corporation.

Niazi wrote poetry in both Urdu and Punjabi. He may be read as a major imagist poet. He used nostalgia, dreams and fantasies as his basic poetic material. His short poems have appealed to a large section of readers as intimate whispers, remarkable for their immediacy of appeal. Niazi evolved a light idiom, a humble tone, and an organic form, eminently suited to his short and pithy poems. As testaments of innocence and beauty, his poems have stayed in the common imagination of his readers for long. Poems from his seven anthologies, some of them being *Tez Hawaa aur Tanha Phool*, *Jungle Mein Dhanak*, *Dushmanon ke Darmiyaan Shaam* and *Maah-e Munir*, are put together in *Kulliyat-e Munir Niazi*.

I

Uga sabza dar-o-deewaar per aahista aahista
Hua khaali sadaaon se nagar aahista aahista

Ghira baadal khamoshi se, khizaan aasaar baaghon mein
Hile thhandi hawaaon mein shajar aahista aahista

Chamak zar ki use aakhir makaan-e khaak mein laai
Banaayaa naag ne jismon mein ghar aahista aahista

Mere baahar faseelein theen ghubaar-e khaak-o baaran ki
Mili mujh ko tere ghum ki khabar aahista aahista

Munir is mulk per aasaib ka saaya hai ya kya hai
Ke harkat tez tar hai aur safar aahista aahista

I

The green grass showed up on the walls, bit by bit
The city got shorn of echoes, bit by bit

Clouds gathered in silence, by the ruined orchards
The cool breeze then shook the boughs, bit by bit

The lure of riches brought him to abode of dust
The snakes made their way in limbs, bit by bit

The screens of dust and wind lay beyond my being
I got to know of your pain and plight, bit by bit

Does an evil spirit haunt my land, Munir
The speed is fast but journey slow, bit by bit

2

Meri saari zindagi ko be-samar us ne kiya
'Umr meri thee magar us ko basar us ne kiya

Main bahut kamzor tha is mulk mein hijrat ke baad
Per mujhe is mulk mein kamzor tar us ne kiya

Raahbar mera banaa gumraah karne ke liye
Mujh ko seedhe raste se dar-ba-dar us ne kiya

Shahr mein wo mutabar meri gawaahi se hua
Phir mujhe is shahr mein na-mutabar us ne kiya

Shahr ko barbaad kar ke rakh diya us ne Munir
Shahr per ye zulm mere naam per us ne kiya

2

Who rendered all my life meaningless, but only he
This life was mine, who lived this life, but only he

Too frail I was, too frail, in this land on migration
He made me frailer still, who else, but only he

He became the way finder only to put me astray
Who led me away from the right way, but only he

My witness alone stood by him in his city
I was proved fake, who made me so, but only he

He ruined this city Munir, beyond all repair
In my name, who ruined the city, but only he

38

Zeb Ghauri

Zeb Ghauri (1928–1985) was born Khan Ahmad Hussain Khan Ghauri. He hailed from Kanpur, Uttar Pradesh, and lived there pursuing his vocation as a poet, with sincere commitment towards discovering a voice and a technique of his own. He belonged to the group of poets who rose to prominence with the modernist movement, gaining momentum and critical recognition during the late 1960s and early '70s. He is one of those poets who came to stay on even after the ultra-modernists started losing their fire and settled down to speak in quieter tones using sober modes of expression.

Ghauri is clearly recognizable among his contemporaries for his detached yet essentially personal and sympathetic understanding of life's ambiguities and incongruities. He published his ghazals in a collection titled *Zard Zarkhaiz*. His second collection, *Chaak*, was published posthumously in Pakistan.

I

Shahr mein hum se kuchh aashufta dilaan aur bhi hain
Sahil-e bahr pe qadmon ke nishaan aur bhi hain

Ret ke toode chamak uthh'te hain jab zulmat mein
Aisa lagta hai ke kuchh log yahaan aur bhi hain

Kaise manzar the ke sheeshe ki tarah toot gaye
Magar aankhon mein kaee khwab-e giraan aur bhi hain

Bastiyaan dil ki bhi sunsaan padi hain kab se
Ye khandar hi naheen saayon ke makaan aur bhi hain

Shub ke sannate mein chattanon ko dekho ai Zeb
Tum se begana-i faryyad-o fughaan aur bhi hai

I

The city has some more anguished ones, not only me
Some more footprints on the seashore, not only mine

The sand dunes shine bright when it grows pitch dark
Seems the place has more like me, not only me

What sights were those to crush like frail glasses
But I've more of dear dreams, not only those

The heart has stayed deserted all along
There are more abodes for shadows, not only these

Look at the rocks in the quiet of night, Zeb
There are more who don't wail, not only you

2

Ho chuke gum saare khadd-o khaal manzar aur main
Phir hue ek aasmaan saahil samunder aur main

Ek harf-e raaz dil per aaeena hota hua
Ek kuhar chhaayi hui manzar ba manzar aur main

Chhed kar jaise guzar jaati hai dosheeza hawa
Der se khaamosh hai gehra samunder aur main

Kis qadar ek doosre se lagte hain maanoos Zeb
Naariyal ke ped ye saahil ke pathhar aur main

2

All outlines are lost, all sights, all landscapes and me
  They're one again—the sky, sea, shore, and me

    A secret word being a mirror to the heart
    A haze spread from scene to scene, and me

    As the maiden wind teases when it passes on
    But silent for so long are the deep sea, and me

    How well known they are to each other, Zeb!
  Those coconut trees, these stones on shore, and me

39

Jaun Eliya

Jaun Eliya (1931–2002), generally described as a philosopher, rebel, radical, atheist and a holder of an offbeat political stance, was born in Amroha, India. Following the 1947 Partition, he migrated to Pakistan and came into prominence as a poet on account of his intriguingly individual approach to poetic diction and syntax. He was proficient in Arabic, Persian, Sanskrit and English, as well as Hebrew which he could access to a limited extent. Eliya was deeply interested in philosophy, logic, Islamic history, Sufism and Kabaala, which is well borne out by the kind of poetry he wrote to express his despair and deep-rooted frustration.

As Eliya was not quite convinced about publishing his poetry, his first book, *Shaayad*, appeared when he was sixty. Other collections of his poetry including *Yaani*, *Gumnaam*,

Lekin and *Goya* were published posthumously. Unlike any other poet, Eliya emerged as a cult figure with a large following in India and Pakistan. He edited a journal called *Insha* and also published essays and translations of Sufi, Mutazilite and Ismaili treatises. In recognition of his contribution to Urdu poetry, the government of Pakistan conferred upon him the prestigious Pride of Performance award. Eliya died in Karachi.

I

Hum jee rahe hain koee bahaana kiye baghair
Us ke baghair us ki tamanna kiye baghair

Ambaar us ka parda-i hurmat banaa miyan
Deewar tak giri naheen parda kiye baghair

Yaaraan wo jo hai mera maseeha-i jaan-o dil
Behad azeez hai mujhe achha kiye baghair

Main bistar-e-khayaal pe letaa hoon us ke paas
Subh-e azal se koee taqaaza kiye baghair

Us ka hai jo bhi kuchh hai mera aur main magar
Wo mujh ko chahiye koee sauda kiye baghair

Ye zindagi jo hai use maani bhi chaahiye
Waada hamein qubool hai eefa kiye baghair

Ai qaatilon ke shahr bus itni hi 'arz hai
Main hoon na qatl koee tamaasha kiye baghair

Murshid ke jhoot ki to sazaa behisaab hai
Tum chhodiyo na shahr ko sehra kiye baghair

Un aanganon mein kitna sukoon-o suroor tha
Aaraaish-e nazar teri parwa kiye baghair

Girya kunan ki fard mein apna naheen hai naam
Hum girya kun azal ke hain girya kiye baghair

Aakhir hain kaun log jo bakhshe hi jaaenge
Taareekh ke haraam se tauba kiye baghair

I

I live on, but without ever making a plea
Without her, without even a desire for her

The rubbish became its veil of pride, my dear
Even the wall didn't fall, without drawing a veil

Friends, she that is my messiah of love and life
I dearly love her, without her giving me a cure

I lie next to her on the grand couch of thoughts
To the eternal dawn, without making a claim

What all I have is her's, only her's, but I
I want but only her, without a bargain

This life! This life calls for a meaning indeed
I'll make a promise, without meeting any

O city of assassins! Let me only urge
Let me not be killed, without me doing some fun

The penance for this guide's lies is infinite indeed
Don't you leave the town, without turning it to wild

How cool and blissful were those inner courtyards
O ornamented glance, without a care for you

My name does not figure in the list of mourners
I'm a timeless mourner, without ever mourning

Who are those after all to be granted forgiveness
Without a penitence for sinning against history

2

Jaao qaraar-e be dilaan shaam bakhair shab bakhair
Sehn hua dhuaan dhuaan shaam bakhair shab bakhair

Sham-e wisaal hai qareeb subh-e kamaal hai qareeb
Phir na rahenge sargaraan shaam bakhair shab bakhair

Wajd karegi zindagi jism-ba-jism jaan-ba-jaan
Jism-ba-jism jaan-ba-jaan shaam bakhair shab bakhair

Ai mere shauq ki umang mere shabaab ki tarang
Tujh pe shafaq ka saaibaan shaam bakhair shab bakhair

Tu meri shaairi main hai rang taraaz gulfishaan
Teri bahaar be-khazaan shaam bakhair shab bakhair

Tera khayal khwab khawb khalwat-e jaan ki aab-o taab
Jism jameel-o naujawaan shaam bakhair shab bakhair

Hai mera naam arjumand tera hisaar sarbaland
Banu-i shahr-e jism-o jaan shaam bakhair shab bakhair

Deed se jaan-e deed tak dil se rukh-e umeed tak
Koee naheen hai darmiyaan shaam bakhair shab bakhair

Ho gaee dair jao tum mujh ko gale lagao tum
Tu meri jaan hai meri jaan shaam bakhair shab bakhair

Sham bakhair shab bakhair mauj-e shamim-e pairhan
Teri mehak rahegi yaan shaam bakhair shab bakhair

2

Go away, patience of the heartless one; good evening, good night
The yard is wrapped in smoke all about; good evening,
good night

The dusk of union is here; the dawn of perfection nearby
No longer would the smoke hang heavy; good evening,
good night

Life will dance an euphoric dance, body by body, breath by breath
Body by body and breath by breath; good evening, good night

You, the zeal and zest of life; you, the cadence of my youth
May you rest in twilight's tent; good evening, good night

You enliven my poetry, colour-spread, petal-blown
Your spring without an autumn; good evening, good night

Your thoughts, a fair of dazzling dreams, a shine of union
Body-beautiful, body-blazing; good evening, good night

My stature so exalted, your fences so head-high
Lady of soul's and body's city; good evening, good night

From eye to pupil of eye, from heart to brink of hope
There is none in-between; good evening, good night

It is late; you must leave now, come close, embrace awhile
You are my love—my life—my love; good evening, good night

Swing of her garment's aroma; good evening, good night
Your whiff will stay all alive; good evening, good night

40

Ahmad Faraz

Ahmad Faraz (1931–2008) is the nom de plume of Syed Ahmad Shah, who was born at Kohat in Pakistan. He moved to Peshawar and acquired his master's degrees in Urdu and Persian literatures. He later joined Peshawar University as a faculty member. In the subsequent years, Faraz worked as a radio producer. Along with his professional engagements, he also wrote poems with political leanings, which landed him in trouble during the regime of General Zia-ul-Haq. He spent some years in countries outside Pakistan and his reputation as an extremely popular poet travelled far beyond and reached new spaces. On his return home, he was appointed as the director general of *Lok Virsa*, the chairman of Pakistan Academy of Letters and also of National Book Foundation. Faraz earned three prestigious awards—Hilaal-e Imtiaaz, Sitaar-i Imtiaaz and finally, Hilaal-e Pakistan from the government of Pakistan.

Faraz is generally classed as a poet of romance, love and finer human passions, who expressed himself in soft, lyrical and dialogic modes. However, his poetry of protest is no less significant. His poetry has been widely translated and put to music. A prolific poet, he has left behind fourteen collections of his poetry: *Tanhaa Tanhaa, Dard Aashob, Naayaaft, Khwaab-e Gul Pareshaan Hai, Bodlak, Shab Khoon, Mere Khwaab Reza Reza, Naabeena Shahr Mein Aaeena, Pus Andaaz Mausam, Jaanaan Jaanaan, Be-Awaaz Gali Kuchon Mein, Sab Aawaazein Meri Hain, Ghazal Bahaana Karoon* and *Ay Ishq Junoon Pesha*. His major works were collected in *Shahr-e Sukhan Aaraastaa Hai*.

I

Jis samt bhi dekhoon nazar aata hai ke tum ho
Ai jaan-e jahaan ye koee tum sa hai ke tum ho

Ye khwaab hai khushboo hai ke jhonkaa hai ke pal hai
Ye dhund hai baadal hai ke saaya hai ke tum ho

Is deed ki saa'at mein kaee rang hain larzaan
Main hoon ke koee aur hai dunya hai ke tum ho

Dekho ye kisee aur ki aankhein hain ke meri
Dekhoon ye kisee aur ka chehra hai ke tum ho

Ye 'umr-e gurezaan kaheen thhehre to ye janoon
Har saans mein mujh ko yehi lagta hai ke tum ho

Har bazm mein mauzoo-e sukhan dil zadagaan ka
Ab kaun hai, Shireen hai ke Laila hai ke tum ho

Ek dard ka phaila hua sehra hai ke main hoon
Is mauj main aayaa hua darya hai ke tum ho

Vo waqt na aai ke dil-e zaar bhi soche
Is shahr mein tanha koi hum saa hai ke tum ho

Aabaad hum aashuftaa saron se naheen maqtal
Ye rasm abhi shahr mein zinda hai ke tum ho

Ai jan-e Faraz itni bhi taufeeq kise thee
Hum ko gham-e hasti bhi gawaara hai ke tum ho

I

Wherever I look, I see only you
Love! Is that one like you, or only you

A dream, a fragrance, a whiff of air, a moment
Some mist, or cloud, or reflection, or only you

Many a shade shivers in a moment of your glimpse
Me, or someone else; this very world, or only you

See if they are someone else's eyes, or only mine
See if this is someone else's face, or only you

May this voyage of life stop; may I then surmise—
Every passing breath whispers: this is only you

In each assembly, the only words lovers repeat:
Is that Shireen, is that Laila, or only you?

Is that the wilderness of pain, or is that me?
A river in the course of surge, or only you

May not the time come for my poor heart to ponder
Is that lonesome one, one like me, or only you

The altar isn't aglow with the wild ones like us
What remains alive—this custom, or only you

Dear Faraz! None has the courage to bear but I
Bear all the pains of life for none, but only you

2

Is daur-e be-junoon ki kahaani koee likho
Jimson ko barf khoon ko paani koee likho

Koee kaho ke haath qalam kis tarah hue
Kyun ruk gaee qalam ki rawaani koee likho

Kyun ahl-e shauq sar-o garebaan hain dosto
Kyun khoon ba dil hai ahd-e jawaani koee likho

Kyun surma dar gulu hai har ek taair-e sukhan
Kyun gulsitaan qafas ka hai saani koee likho

Haan taazaa sanehon ka kare kaun intezaar
Haan dil ki waardaat puraani koee likho

2

The tale of the tamed times, let someone write
Body—ice, blood—water, let someone write

How were those hands chopped off, let someone say!
Why did the flowing pen stop, let someone write!

Why have the company keepers drawn apart now?
Why is the youth blood-smeared, let someone write!

Why is every bird sad and silent now?
Why is the garden like a cage, let someone write!

So, why should one wait for a fresh blow yet?
Just an old tale of heart, let someone write

41

Bani

Bani (1932–1981) was born Rajinder Manchada in Multan, but as the 1947 Partition pushed families across borders, young Bani too had to migrate and find a home in Delhi. He completed his education with a master's degree in economics. He spent all his life teaching in a school in Delhi and pursuing the vocation of poetry passionately. He lived a life of disease and suffering, but showed unique perseverance to sustain all odds. He took care of his ill health to sustain his job for a living and pursue his vocation as a poet.

Bani broke fresh ground in writing his ghazals which had already been liberated from the romantic notions of love, life, and the stereotypes of art. He evolved a diction that was wholly new in its exploitation of the common speech. His metaphors were drawn from the world and the nature around, which he approached with complete clinical detachment. Two of his collections, *Harf-e M'utabar* and *Hisaab-e Rang*, were published during his lifetime, while the third one, *Shafaq Shajar*, was published posthumously. Bani also wrote prose and his works showed his fresh and critical perspective on some of his contemporary Urdu writers.

I

Hari sunehri khaak udaane waala main
Shafaq shajar tasweer banaane waala main

Khala ke saare rang sametne waali shaam
Shab ki mizha pe khwaab sajaane waala main

Fiza ka pehla phool khilaane waali sub'ha
Hawa ke sur mein geet milaane waala main

Baahar bheeter fasl ugaane waala too
Tere khazaane sadaa lutaane waala main

Chhaton pe baarish, door pahaadi, halki dhoop
Bheegne waalaa, pankh sukhaane waala main

Chaar dishaaein jab aapas mein ghul mil jaaein
Sannate ko dua banaane waala main

Ghane banon mein shankh bajaane waalaa too
Teri taraf ghar chhod ke aane waala main

I

Who blows the green and golden dust—none else but me
Who paints the glowing skies and boughs—none else but me

Who gathers the hues of the horizon—none else but dusk
Who decks the night's eyelashes with dreams—none else
but me

Who helps the first blossoms to life—none else but the dawn
Who sings a song to the wind's tune—none else but me

Who fills the entire flora with life—none else but you
Who squanders all your treasures—none else but me

Rains on terrace, hills far off, and the sun so mild
Who soaks in rain, who dries up feathers—none else but me

When the four directions meet, when they merge in one
Who turns the frozen hush to prayer—none else but me

Who blows the conch shell in deep jungles—none else
but you
Who leaves the abode and comes to you—none else but me

2

Ali bin Muttaqi roya
Wahi chup tha wahi roya

Ajeeb ashob irfaan mein
Fizaa gum thee ke ji roya

Yaqeen mismaar mausam ka
Khandar khud hi tahi roya

Azaan zeena utar aayi
Sukoot-e baatini roya

Khalaa har zaat ke undar
Sunaa jis ne wahi roya

Sehar dum kaun rotaa hai
Ali bin Muttaqi roya

2

Ali bin Muttaqi wept
Only he was silent, he wept

In painful dawn of wisdom
Climes were aghast, the heart wept

So, faith-broken, weather-worn
For their losses, the ruins wept

Prayers' call came downstairs
Then the inner silence wept

A void inside every being
Whoever heard only wept

Who weeps at the dawn's break but
Ali bin Muttaqi wept

42

Zafar Iqbal

Zafar Iqbal (1932–) was born in Bahawalnagar, Pakistan. He was a lawyer by profession but also served in between as the director general of the Urdu Science Board, Lahore. He emerged as one of the most prominent and unusual voices of the Urdu ghazal although his contribution has also been debated upon sometimes.

Iqbal dislodged the old values of poetry with a bang. One can say that his poetry emerged as an ultra-modernist variation on modernism that took time to be accepted as yet another way of writing. His innovations lay especially in the domain of diction. He developed a new poetic syntax at a time when poetry in Urdu had started making bold experiments with form and language. His experimentations went through phases of extremity and moderation, as he tried to test the limits of language and diction to contain the pressures of experiences that were more mundane than sublime and more rebellious than prescriptive. Iqbal's first three collections, *Aab-e Rawaan*, *Gulaaftab* and *Ratb-o Yaabis*, earned him a reputation that strengthened further with the subsequent works. A prolific poet, he continued with his vocation, doing and undoing his poetic practices, and always exploring where his language and his material for poetry lay hidden. His works like *Ratb-o Yaabis*, *Ghubaar Aalood Samton ka Safar*, *Aib-o Hunar*, *Atraaf* and *Wahm-o Gumaan* bear testimony to the fertility of his imagination and creative talent. His poetry has been collected in four volumes under the title *Ab Tak*.

I

Chalo itnee to aasaani rahegi
Milenge aur pareshaani rahegi

Isee se raunaq-e daryaa-i dil hai
Yehi ek lehar toofaani rahegi

Kabhi ye shauq naamaanoos hoga
Kabhi wo shakl anjaani rahegi

Nikal jaaegi soorat aaeene se
Hamaare ghar mein hairaani rahegi

Subuk sar ho ke jeena hai koee din
Abhi kuchh din giraan jaani rahegi

Sunoge lafz mein bhi phadphdaahat
Lahoo mein bhi pur afshaani rahegi

Hamaari garm guftaari ke baawasf
Hawaa itni hi barfaani rahegi

Abhi dil ki siyaahi zor per hai
Abhi chehre pe taabaani rahegi

Zafar main shahr mein aa to gayaa hoon
Meri khaslat bayaabaani rahegi

I

Well, this much would be welcome
We shall meet though remain glum

This stream would forever flow
Will keep the heart's brook in glow

At times, a craving unknown
At times, that face will bemoan

The mirror will have no face to show
In this house wonders will grow

Life in disgrace, a while more
That is what lies in store

Even in words, a flutter
Blood's gurgle would then utter

In spite of heated words twice
Winds will blow as cold as ice

Heart's gloom grows more gloom still
Faces don't show any chill

I've come to city, Zafar, though
My wild nature will remain so

2

Khaamshi achhee naheen inkaar honaa chaahiye
Ye tamaasha ab sar-e baazaar honaa chaahiye

Khwaab ki tabeer per israar hai jin ko abhee
Pehle un ko khwab se bedaar honaa chaahiye

Doob kar marna bhi asloob-e mohabbat ho to ho
Wo jo darya hai to usko paar honaa chaahiye

Ab wahi karne lage deedaar se aage ki baat
Jo kabhi kehte the bus deedaar honaa chaahiye

Dosti ke naam per keeje na kyunkar dushmani
Kuchh na kuchh aakhir tareeq-e kaar honaa chaahiye

Jhoot bola tha to qayam hi raho us per Zafar
Aadmi ko sahib-e kirdaar hona honaa chaahiye

2

Silence is no good, let there be a negation
Let this show be shown in an open location

If you insist to interpret the dreams' numbers
You should first get out of your own slumbers

Dying drowned may be a lover's cherished dream
If a river, he should cross over the stream

They once said that love's glance would make the day
They now ask for so much more than they may

Why not be a foe in the garb of a friend?
Let there be a way to make an amend

If you spoke a lie, Zafar, stick to your lie
Men would do well, if they could only try

43

Ahmad Mushtaq

Ahmad Mushtaq (1933–) was born in Amritsar, India. He received his early education at home before joining school. Soon after he passed his ninth-standard examination, communal riots broke out. A month after the Partition, he migrated to Lahore from where he passed his matriculation examination. He developed a keen association with some of the poets and writers, during his visits to Pakistan Tea House, who later emerged as serious poets and men of letters in Pakistan. Mushtaq migrated to the United States of America at the age of fifty-one. He worked for the Chartered Bank until his retirement, and has continued living there since then.

Mushtaq's poetry is a silent escape from traditional poetics. He drew upon commonplace images and feelings and described them in an idiom characteristically ordinary and commonplace. He looked at images and objects as they appeared, but added an element of surprise to them. His air, earth, water and sky, towns, houses, lanes and places, are all real, and he responds to them quite naturally. He makes no deliberate comments; he only narrates a common condition but shocks the reader with his strikingly different perception. His first two collections were entitled *Majmua* and *Gard-e Mehtaab*. His collected poems were published in Pakistan as *Kulliyaat-e Ahmad Mushtaq* after his migration to the US. These, along with his later works, were put into one volume and published in India titled *Kulliyaat*. Mushtaq has also edited a volume on Nasir Kazmi called *Hijr ki Raat Ka Sitaara*.

I

Ye kehna to naheen kaafi ke bus pyare lage hum ko
Unhein kaise bataaein hum ke wo kaise lage hum ko

Makeen the ya kisee khoee huee jannat ki tasweerein
Makaan is shahr ke bhule hue sapne lage hum ko

Hum un ko soch mein gum dekh kar waapas palat aai
Wo apne dhyan mein baithhe hue achhe lage hum ko

Bahut shaffaf the jab tak ke masroof-e tamanna the
Magar is kaar-e dunya mein bade dhabbe lage hum ko

Jahaan tanha hue dil mein bhanwar se padne lagte hain
Agarche muddatein guzreen kinaare se lage hum ko

I

Not enough to say how lovely she looked like
How shall I tell her now how good she looked like

They were dwellers, or images of lost heavens
Like the lost dreams, abodes of the city looked like

I saw her lost in deep thoughts, I withdrew myself
Lost in her own thoughts, I loved what she looked like

I was transparent when I nursed my dear dreams
I bore many a blot in life, a blot I looked like

When I get lonely, whirlpools ensnare my heart though
Long back I reached my shore and a torn one I looked like

2

Ye tanha raat ye gehri fizaaein
Use dhoondein ke us ko bhool jaaein

Khayaalon ki ghani khaamoshiyon mein
Ghuli jaati hain lafzon ki sadaaein

Ye raste rahrawon se bheegte hain
Yahaan chhup chhup ke chalti hain hawaaein

Ye paani khaamshi se beh raha hai
Ise dekhein ke is mein doob jaaein

Jo gham jalte hain sheron ki chita main
Unhein phir apne seene se lagaein

Chalo aisa makaan aabaad kar lein
Jahan logon ki aawaazein na aaein

2

This lonely night, this thick air around
Shall I look for her, or keep aground

In dense silence, thoughts don't evolve
The tones of voice can only dissolve

These paths keep the passers-by at bay
Only in hiding the winds can play

This water flows quietly in silence
Shall I watch, or drown in silence

My pains burn on the pyre of verse
Let me embrace them, let me nurse

Let us go and enliven a house
Where no human voices can espouse

44

Mazhar Imam

Mazhar Imam (1933–2012) was born in Darbhanga, Bihar. Following his early education at home, he acquired a diploma from the Film and Television Institute of India, Pune. Later, he got his master's degree in Urdu from Magadh University, Bodh Gaya, and also in Persian from Bihar University, Muzaffarpur. Imam began his professional career as a journalist, editing and writing for at least six publications, some of the more important ones being *Kaarvaan* and *Azad Hind* published from Calcutta. Relinquishing journalism, he became a schoolteacher for some time, and then joined the All India Radio. After working at several places, he retired as the Director, Doordarshan, from Kashmir. Finally, he settled down in Noida, where he breathed his last. Imam has been a recipient of several awards from literary and other organizations including the Sahitya Akademi.

Imam was aware of the traditions of Urdu poetry, including those propounded by the Progressive poets, which he respected while tracking his own route as a poet. He was a poet of romantic disposition but assessed the nature of modernist poetry with a critical eye. He found his space in the act of juxtaposing the past with the present, fancy with reality, contemporary idiom with the classical. In founding a new form for the ghazal called *aazaad*, or free ghazal, he made an innovative move against the very nature of the ghazal itself. His four collections of poetry are *Zakhm-e Tamanna*, *Rishta Goonge Safar Ka*, *Pichhle Mausam Ka Phool* and *Bund Hota Hua Darwaaza*. His ghazals have been collected in *Paalaki Kehkashaan Ki Aati Jaati Lehrein*, *Azaad Ghazal Ka Manzarnama*, *Jameel Mazhari* and *Ek Lehar Aati Hui* form his critical works. His sketches and memoirs are put together in *Aksar Yaad Aate Hain*.

I

Zindagi khwaahish-e baatil hai mera saath na chhod
Tu hi ek umr ka haasil hai mera saath na chhod

Log milte hain sar-e raah guzar jaate hain
Tu hi ek hamsafar-e dil hai mera saath na chhod

Tu ne socha hai mujhe tu ne sanwaara hai mujhe
Tu mera zehn mera dil hai mera saath na chhod

Tu na hoga to kahaan jaa ke jaloonga shab bhar
Tujh se hi garmi-e mehfil hai mera saath na chhod

Main ke biphre hue toofan mein hoon lehron lehron
Tu ke asooda-i saahil hai mera saath na chhod

Is rifaaqat ko sapar apni banaa lein jee lein
Shahr ka shahr hi qaatil hai mera saath na chchod

Ek main ne hi ugaai nahi khwaabon ke gulaab
Tu bhi is jurm mein shaamil hai mera saath na chhod

Ab kisee raah pe jalte nahi chaahat ke chiraagh
Tu meri aakhri manzil hai mera saath na chhod

I

What's this life but a vain desire; don't ever leave me alone
Who else but only you—my life's worth—don't ever
leave me alone

People pass me by on the way; they pass me by to make their way
Who else but only you—my love—don't ever leave me alone

You have spared me a thought; only you have made me what I am
Who else but only you—my head, my heart—don't ever leave
me alone

Where shall I burn all this night, where shall I ever go
without you
Who else but only you—my life, my blood—don't ever leave
me alone

I'm there in each wave—only I'm there in the tempestuous seas
You have kissed the seashore though; don't ever leave me all
alone

Let this camaraderie be my shield, let me live this life in love
The towns around have turned unkind, don't ever leave me alone

I have not nursed my dreams alone; you too have grown the
same crop
As you have grown the same crop, don't ever leave me alone

The paths of love are all deserted; the signs of love nowhere
in sight
Who else but only you—my only goal—don't ever leave me alone

311

2

(Aazaad Ghazal)

Saraasar us pe tuhmat hai ke us ne mujh se kuchh rishta nahi rakkha
Jahaan ke kaar-e gham bakhshe, mujhe tanha naheen rakhha

Tamaazat mehr-e imkaan ki kuchh itni khush murawwat thee
Shajar hum ne lagaaya ghar ke aangan mein, magar saaya naheen rakhha

Raheen bekhanamaan sub nekiyaan apni
Khuda ne mere raste mein koee darya naheen rakhha

Hamein sub rang us ke zahr lagte hain
Zamaane ko shikaayat hai ke hum ne apni aankhon per koee parda naheen rakhha

Samundar se guhar laana bahut mushkil na tha lekin
Hameen ne apni kashti ko jazeere se nikalne ka koee rasta naheen rakhha

Nashe mein khush gumaan-e sub'ha the itne
Kisi ne zakhm-e shub per aaj tak phaaha naheen rakhha

Ek anjaani sadaa kaanon se takraaegi
Diya le kar chale hum phir khayaal aaya ke hum ne ghar mein darwaaza naheen rakhha

2

(A free ghazal)

It's a sheer blame that my love did not keep me company
She blessed me with many a pain, she did keep me company

The warmth of that care was so heart-warming
I grew a plant in my courtyard, but did not keep a shade
for company

All my goodness was in vain
For my God didn't keep a river on my way for company

I consider all her colours my eyes' curse
The world complains: I didn't keep a veil on my eyes
for company

It wasn't difficult to find a pearl from the seas
But for getting my boat out of the island, I didn't keep a
way for company

Those seekers of dawn were so drunk
For the night's wound, no one ever kept a healing touch
for company

An unknown voice struck my ears
I came with a lamp but remembered I hadn't made a door in
the house for company

45

Shakeb Jalali

Shakeb Jalali (1934–1966) was born Syed Hassan Rizvi at a small place called Jalali, near Aligarh, Uttar Pradesh. He passed his matriculation examination from Badayun, Uttar Pradesh. Following the Partition of India and the loss of his parents, he migrated to Rawalpindi with his sister. Jalali continued his education in Rawalpindi, Sialkot and Lahore to acquire his degrees upto the graduation level. He lived a life of economic deprivation and severe emotional stress. He worked for weekly and monthly journals to sustain himself. Unable to put up with his stress any further, Jalali committed suicide by lying down on a railway track in Sargodha at the age of thirty-two, leaving the literary world bereft of a voice that had every potential to hold a prominent place in the canon of modern Urdu poetry.

Jalali's influence on the Urdu literary scenario, even five decades after his death, establishes him as a poet of lasting value. Elements of deprivation, pain, and man's inability to reach a desired destination marked his poetry. He discovered a philosophical stance in portraying these sentiments, and spoke with a sense of pride and confidence, rather than loss and deprivation. His collections, *Raushni Ai Raushni* and *Kulliyaat-e Shakeb Jalali,* were published posthumously.

I

Gale mila na kabhi chaand bakht aisa tha
Hara bhara badan apna darakht jaisa tha

Sitaare siskiyaan bharte the os roti thi
Fasana-i jigar-e lakht lakht aisaa tha

Zaraa na mom hua pyar ki haraarat se
Chatakh ke toot gaya dil ka sakht aisa tha

Ye aur baat ke wo lub the phool se naazuk
Koee na seh sake lehja karakht aisa tha

Kahaan ki sair na kee tausan-e takhayyul pe
Hamein to ye bhi Sulaiman ke takht jaisa tha

Idhar se guzra tha mulk-e sukhan ka shahzaada
Koee na jaan saka saaz-o rakht aisa tha

I

The moon didn't embrace me ever; I had no luck
My body was a lush tree but not moonstruck

The stars sobbed, the dewdrop shed a tear
My poor heart's tale too was none of cheer

The warmth of pure love could never melt
The hardened heart cracked but never knelt

Lips more delicate than a flower petal
But her harsh tone showed its real mettle

I roamed on the wings of imagination
That was Solomon's throne of high station

The prince of muses had passed this way
None could know who he was, none could say

2

Jahaan talak bhi ye sehra dikhaayi deta hai
Meri tarah se akela dikhaayi deta hai

Na itni tez chale sarphiri hawa se kaho
Shajar pe ek hi patta dikhaayi deta hai

Bura na maaniye logon ki aib jooee ka
Unhein to din ko bhi saaya dikhaayi deta hai

Ye aik abr ka tukda kahaan kahaan barse
Tamaam dasht hi pyasa dikhaayi deta hai

Wahein pahunch ke giraaenge badbaan ab to
Wo door koee jazeera dikhaayi deta hai

Meri nigaah se chhup kar kahaan rahega koee
Ke ab to sung bhi sheesha dikhaayi deta hai

Simat ke rah gaye aakhir pahaad se qad bhi
Zameen se har koee ooncha dikhaayi deta hai

Khili hai dil mein kisee ke badan ki dhoop Shakeb
Har aik phool sunehra dikhaayi deta hai

2

To the farthest end of wilderness, if you may see
Lonesome like me is this wilderness, if you may see

Tell the brusque wind, tell not to blow so very hard
That's the only leaf on the bole, if you may see

Don't ever feel so bad if people find faults with you
They see shadows even in daylight, if you may see

A single piece of cloud and many a cracked earth
Entire wilderness looks thirsty, if you may see

We shall fold our flags, but only when we reach there
There lies an island somewhere there, if you may see

Who can hide from my view, who can live in hiding
Now, the stone looks like a glass, if you may see

Even the tall ones that stood like mounts have shrunk
Now each one looks taller than earth, if you may see

Someone's body's radiance fills my heart, Shakeb
Now every blossom is aglow, if you may see

46

Zehra Nigah

Zehra Nigah (1935–) was born in Hyderabad, India, but she migrated to Pakistan following the 1947 Partition. She grew up in a distinguished family with a well-pruned taste for literature and culture. This gave her an opportunity to come across some major writers of the time, and take her first lessons in literature and literary writing quite early in life.

Inspired essentially by the Urdu classical poets, Nigah initiated her poetic career by writing the poetry of romantic themes with certain lyric grace. Soon, she distinguished herself for two basic reasons: first, her ability to voice female experiences, and second, her socio-political outlook which found fuller expressions in her ghazals and nazms. She also asserted her historical significance in the way she emerged as a powerful female voice, along with Ada Jafarey, at a time when women's writing was placed on the margins. In making her aspirations known, she projected an alternative view of domesticity and femininity in a male-dominated literary space, which set a precedent. She viewed familial themes, images and personages from her own perspective, and expressed them in a diction that represented a clear female tone of voice. Her significance lies in the way she liberated the personal and the political, in and outside her country, and imparted them the authenticity of a poet's vision. Nigah is widely considered an iconic female figure, who wrote poetry as well as scripts for TV serials, won awards, and made her place with her three collections, namely, *Shaam Ka Pehla Taara*, *Waraq* and *Firaaq*.

I

Der tak raushni rahi kal raat
Main ne odhi thi chandani kal raat

Aik muddat ke baad dhund chhati
Dil ne apni kahi suni kal raat

Ungliyaan aasmaan chhooti theen
Haan meri dastras mein thi kal raat

Uthh'ta jaataa tha pardai-i-nisyaan
Ek ek baat yaad thi kal raat

Taaq-e dil pe thi ghunghruon ki sada
Ek jhadi see lagi rahi kal raat

Jugnuon ke se lamhe ud'te the
Meri muthhi main aa gaee kal raat

I

The light stayed for long last night
I was wrapped in moonlight last night

The fog melted after a long time
And the heart told its tale last night

My fingers touched the sky high
The sky was in reach last night

Oblivion's veil got lifted
I recalled each event last night

In heart's alcove, jingle bells rang
There was a long drizzle last night

The moments flew as fireflies do
I got them in my fist last night

2

Is raah-e shikasta per aiwaan-e hukoomat kya?
Tukdon ki hai kya qeemat malbe ki hai wus'at kya?

Kaasa liye baithhe hon, maange pe guzaara ho
Ye naaz-e shuja'at kyun ye zaum-e hifaazat kya?

Haakim diye jaate hain ahkaam-e falatooni
Jab lafz hon behurmat aadaab-e ataa'at kya?

Haasil ke nahi saude baazar mein mandi hai
Chal ai dil-e kam maya phir teri bhi qeemat kya?

2

On a road so broken, what's the seat of power?
What's the price of shreds, what's the worth of rubbish?

If one sits with a begging bowl, if one lives on alms
What vanity in power, what pride in protection?

The rulers keep on tossing their noble commands
When words lack value, what manner obedience?

No worth of goods now; no worth in a slumped market
Move, my heart of meagre means, what worth are you?

47

Bashir Badr

Bashir Badr (1935–) is the nom de plume of Syed Mohammad Bashir, who was born in Ayodhya, a place that evokes historical and communal memories of great pride and pain. He received his MA and PhD in Urdu Literature from Aligarh Muslim University, where he also taught before joining Meerut College as a faculty member. Having suffered the onslaughts of communal riots when his house was burnt, he chose to relocate to Bhopal.

Badr shot into prominence in the 1970s, soon after the publication of his first collection of ghazals called *Ekaayee*. His voice was entirely new, his idiom colloquial and commonplace and his imagery effortlessly drawn from the life around. Young men and women, ecstasy and despair, enlivened his compositions. While he continued with his chosen material, he also made effortless experiments with the form of ghazal and gained further ground with his subsequent collections, *Image*,

Aamad, Aasmaan and *Aas*. His mode of address, controlled yet sentimental, ensured an instant place for him in the popular imagination of his readers. He received awards from various literary organizations, travelled widely, in and outside India, to recite his ghazals at houseful mushairas in an inimitable style and sonorous voice. His works have been collected and published in Pakistan as *Kulliyaat-e Bashir Badr*. An academic all his life, Badr also published critical studies of Urdu ghazal since Independence and the modern ghazal of the twentieth century. A poet who ruled the mushaira and literary scenario for decades is now a victim of the Alzheimer's disease.

I

Yaad ab khud ko aa rahe hain hum
Kuchh dinon tak Khuda rahe hain hum

Aaj to apni khaamshi mein bhi
Teri aawaaz paa rahe hain hum

Baat kya hai ke phir zamaane ko
Yaad rah rah ke aa rahe hain hum

Jo kabhi laut kar nahi aate
Wo zamaane bula rahe hain hum

Zindagi ab to saadgi se mil
Baad sadiyon ke aa rahe hain hum

Ab hamein dekh bhi na paaoge
Itne nazdeek aa rahe hain hum

Ghazlein ab tak sharaab peeti theen
Neem ka rus pila rahe hain hum

Dhoop nikli hai muddaton ke baad
Geele jazbe sukha rahe hain hum

I

A God for some time now
I recall myself now

Even in my solitude
I can hear your voice now

What's the matter, why this world?
Remembers me often now

Ages that never return
But I must call them back now

Life! Meet me with no pretence
Ages later, I come now

You wouldn't even see me then
So close I am getting now

Ghazal has been drinking wine
I bring her a bitter drink now

The sun has shown after ages
I dry up moist emotions now

Sardiyon mein lihaaf se chimte
Chand taaron pe ja rahe hain hum

Zeest ki ek barqi ladki ko
Noor Namah padha rahe hain hum

Us ne poochha hamaare ghar ka pata
Coffee house bula rahe hain hum

Kandhe uchka ke baat karne mein
Munfarid hote ja rahe hain hum

Teddy tehzeeb teddy fikr-o nazar
Teddy ghzalein suna rahe hain hum

In hard winter, wrapped in quilt
I leave for the starry skies now

To a life's electrifying lass
I am teaching *Noor Nama* now

He asked me of my address
I take him to coffee house now

I talk with shaking shoulders
I've got so special now

Teddy culture, thoughts and ways
I recite teddy ghazals now

2

Saanp jab os ka badan chaate
Ret ko ret ki jalan chaate

Barf ki ungliyaan agar choomoon
Mere talwon ko ek kiran chaate

Kis mohabbat se choomate ho hamein
Saanp jis tarha apna mun chaate

Ek lamhe ki raushni ke liye
Aag kaaghaz ka pairahan chaate

Ek hazaar ek raat ke phun hain
Jab ye naagin kisee ka tun chaate

Mard us samt dekhte hi naheen
Gaai jab gaai ka badan chaate

Zard kutte ki surkh jeebh kabhi
Surmaee raat ki thakan chaate

2

When a dewdrop the snake licks
Then sand's blaze, the sand licks

If I kiss the snow's fingers
My soul, a ray of sun licks

You kiss me with such pure love
As its own being, the snake licks

To create a moment's light
The paper's garb, the fire licks

Night unfurls a thousand hoods
Someone's body, the snake licks

Men don't look that side ever
When a cow's body, a cow licks

The red tongue of a pale dog
The grey night's exhaustion licks

Ek billi safed choohe ka
Dhoop mein baith kar badan chaate

Ek khargosh barf per leta
Ik gilahree ka sard tun chaate

Aaeena khaane mein akela saanp
Jhoom jhoom aap apna phun chaate

Do minute mein cooker ki saat dishein
Ungliyaan ab ghazal ka fun chaate

A cat, basking in the sun
Of a white rat's body licks

A rabbit lying on snow
A squirrel's cold body licks

Lonely snake in mirror-house
Its own hood, in rapture licks

A cooker, two minutes, seven dishes
Now the art of ghazal, the finger licks

48

Adil Mansuri

Adil Mansuri (1936–2008), poet, painter, calligrapher and playwright, was born Farid Mohammad in Ahmedabad. His mother tongue was Gujarati but he also learnt Arabic and Urdu in Karachi, where his family had migrated after the Partition of India to see if their life could be better there. Returning eight years later to his native land, Mansuri revisited himself afresh as a young man of twenty years. He finally chose to settle down in the United States of America at the age of fifty, where he also breathed his last. He is one of the very few who combined the vocations of calligraphy, painting, digital art, plays and poetry, and used his multiple skills to write avant-garde poetry both in Gujarati and Urdu, and win several awards.

Mansuri belonged to the first line of modernists who made bold interventions in language and form, as his collection, *Hashr Ki Sub'ha Darakhshan Ho*, shows. He used his poetry as a canvas to configure the political and the social, alongside the cultural, contours of his times. He was acutely conscious of contemporary history and Islamic tradition, as also of colour, word and image. Mansuri did not indulge in a conscious construction of meaning; in fact, he broke the constraints of language and meaning to approach the meaning of meaning. He, thus, reached to a supposed meaning through apparent meaninglessness, which in turn, defined him as a surrealist poet of remarkable significance. 'I am curious about shapes, colours, form, light, horizon, time, language, scripts,' he wrote, 'and every day, I move ahead into curiosity, my endless journey.'

I

Ghoorata kya hai kameene kutte
Soonghata kya hai kameene kutte

Chandani odh so gaee basti
Jaagata kya hai kameene kutte

Shab ki khaamoshi sun sake to sun
Bhaunkata kya hai kameene kutte

Ye to teri hi apni haddi hai
Chaata'ta kya hai kameene kutte

Ghair ka aks aaeene mein kahaan
Nochata kya hai kameene kutte

Tere saai ka tujh pe paon pada
Kata'ta kya hai kameene kutte

Teri manzil hunooz koson door
Haanpata kya hai kameene kutte

Saamana kar tamaam dunya ka
Bhagata kya hai kameene kutte

Sochane ka koee 'ilaaj naheen
Sochata kya hai kameene kutte

Dekh saari Khudaaee jaag uthhi
Oonghata kya hai kameene kutte

338

I

(A ghazal that is also a soliloquy)

Why stare, you lowly dog?
Why sniff, you lowly dog?

In moonlight, the village sleeps
Why awake, you lowly dog?

Hear this night's silence, if you can
Why so bark, you lowly dog?

Can't you see your own bone, dog!
Why lick it, you lowly dog?

There is none else in mirror
Why dig it, you lowly dog?

Your shadow stepped over you
Why then bite, you lowly dog?

Your goal still so far away!
Why pant now, you lowly dog?

Face the world squarely now
Why run away, you lowly dog?

No remedy for dark thoughts
Why then think, you lowly dog?

God's creation is awake
Why then doze, you lowly dog?

2

Ruswaayi se ab bacha lo Aleph
Pateele main rakh kar ubaalo Aleph

Badan Bey ke under utar jaai to
Kinaare pe rah kar nikaalo Aleph

Kaheen to kisee shai se takraaegi
Khalaaon mein jaa kar uchhaalo Aleph

Bure waqt mein saath deta hai kaun
Sabhi apne apne sambhaalo Aleph

Kisee ka bhi ho us se kya waasta
Padaa gar mile to uthha lo Aleph

Ye paani to pighli hui barf hai
To sooraj ke haathon sukha lo Aleph

Pighal jaaiga mom ban kar abhi
Andhera hi achha bujha lo Aleph

Lagee hai to basti ko jal jaane do
Magar ho sake to bacha lo Aleph

2

Save me now from this disgrace, Aleph
Put me in the pan, boil Aleph

If the body slides in Bey
Be at the banks, salvage Aleph

It will bump into something
Go into open, toss Aleph

None keeps company in bad times
Let one save one's own Aleph

Don't even bother whose it is
If found lying, grab Aleph

Water is but melted ice
Go to the sun, dry Aleph

It will melt like wax in a while
It's better dark, put out Aleph

Let the village burn, if it burns
If you may save, save Aleph

49

Shahryar

Shahryar (1936–2012), poet, academic and film lyricist, was
born Kunwar Akhlaq Mohammad Khan in Aonla, Uttar
Pradesh. He received his early education in Bulandshahr,
before joining Aligarh Muslim University for higher studies.
He began his professional career with Anjumn Tarraqi Urdu,
and then left it to join his alma mater as a faculty member.
Shahryar built up his reputation as an academic and poet,
who later wrote some memorable lyrics for films without ever
compromising with his literary criterion or taste. He also edited
Sher-O Hikmat, a literary journal of lasting value, with another
academic fellow, Mughni Tabassum. Shahryar's popularity with
both literary and common readers kept him in the forefront for
decades. He received the Sahitya Akademi Award as also the
most prestigious Jnanpeeth Award.

Shahryar's poetry is marked by a sense of bewilderment and intellectual curiosity. With an acute sensitivity to the classical forms of ghazal writing, he evolved an idiom for his compositions through an artful absorption of traditions, rather than an outright denial of older values. He is considered to have contributed significantly to the development of the short poem in Urdu, marked by metaphoric precision and linguistic ease. His five collections, *Ism-e Aazam, Saatwaan Dar, Hijr Ke Mausam, Khwaab Ka Dar Bund Hai* and *Neend ki Kirchein*, are witness to his gradual growth from a poet of seemingly simple apprehensions of life to a writer with a deep philosophical understanding of life as a phenomenon. Shahryar's collections have also appeared in Devanagari script that bear witness to his popularity among Hindi readers.

I

Zindagi jaisi tawwaqo thi naheen, kuchh kam hai
Har ghadi hotaa hai ehsaas kaheen kuchh kam hai

Ghar ki taameer tasawwur hi mein ho sakti hai
Apne naqshe ke mutaabiq ye zameen kuchh kam hai

Bichhde logon se mulaaqat kabhi phir hogi
Dil mein ummeed to kaafi hai, yaqeen kuchh kam hai

Ab jidhar dekhiye lagtaa hai ke is dunya mein
Kaheen kuchh cheez ziyaada hai kaheen kuchh kam hai

Aaj bhi hai teri doori hi udaasi ka sabab
Ye alag baat ke pehli si naheen kuchh kam hai

I

Life is not as I thought; somewhere, something less
A feeling lingers, there's somewhere, something less

I can surely make a house but only in my dreams
I surely have a map but the space somewhat less

Those who have parted now will surely someday meet
I've enough hope in heart but the faith somewhat less

Wherever you look, the world would look uneven
Something somewhere more, somewhere something less

Even today, I'm sad you've gone so far away
But not as ever, my sadness is somewhat less

2

Zakhmon ko rafoo kar lein dil shaad karein phir se
Khwaabon ki koee dunya aabaad karein phir se

Muddat hui jeene ka ehsaas naheen hota
Dil un se taqaaza kar bedaad karein phir se

Mujrim ke katahre mein phir hum ko khada kar do
Ho rasm-e kohan taaza faryaad karein phir se

Ai ahl-e junoon dekho zanjeer hue saai
Hum kaise unhein socho aazaad karein phir se

Ab jee ke bahalne ki hai ek yahi soorat
Beeti huee kuchh baatein, hum yaad karein phir se

2

Let's stich our wounds, let's make merry once again
Let's find a world of dreams, let's roam it once again

It has been long since I have felt I am alive
Let my heart make a plea, find a way once again

Stand me in dock again, let me pray for mercy
Let those rites follow, let them follow once again

Crazy friends! The chains have now turned to shadows
How can I set them free, how can I, once again?

That's the only way for my heart to seek its cheer
Recall the days gone by and ruminate once again

50

Saqi Farooqi

Saqi Farooqi (1936–2018) was born Qazi Mohammad Shamshad Nabi in Gorakhpur, Uttar Pradesh, from where his family migrated to Bangladesh in 1947, before settling in Pakistan in 1950. A resident of a new world in an age of consequential transformations, Farooqi moved to London in 1958 to work as a computer programmer, although he represents the movements of life and times as a diasporic poet and prose writer of great merit.

Farooqi's individuality lies in his experimentation with the Urdu language, the traditional line lengths of the Urdu verse and the stereotypical rhythm of Urdu diction. Further, he found a new form for these experimentations in a complete denial of the existing form of Urdu poetry. Both his poetry, and remarkably fresh prose, may best be read as narratives free of the drama and melodrama of life. Saqi turns futuristic quite often, as he goes beyond the limits of the modern and the postmodern. He uses language intuitively to incorporate the fragmentary conditions of his time. He turns anecdotal and reflective by turns, representing the mundane and the philosophical in the complex kaleidoscope of his poetry. This iconoclast of the new Urdu nazm and ghazal, has strengthened his poetry with unusual perceptions of the world and the text. This is amply illustrated by his curiously titled collections, *Radar*, *Zindaa Paani Sacchaa* and *Surkh Gulaab Aur Badr-e Muneer*.

I

Wo log jo zinda hain mar jaaenge ik din
Ik raat ke raahi hain guzar jaaenge ik din

Yoon dil mein uthhi lehr yoon aankhon mein bhare rung
Jaise mere haalaat sanwar jaaenge ik din

Dil aaj bhi jalta hai usee tez hawa mein
Ai tez hawa! Dekh bikhar jaaenge ik din

Yoon hai ke ta'aaqub mein hai aasaaish-e dunya
Yoon hai ke muhabbat se bikhar jaaenge ik din

Yoon hoga ke un aankhon se aansoon na bahenge
Ye chaand sitare bhi theher jaaenge ik din

Ab ghar bhi naheen ghar ki tamanna bhi naheen hai
Muddat huee socha tha ke ghar jaaenge ik din

I

All those who live now will die one day
Travellers of a night will fly one day

My heart has waves, my eyes have colours
As if I'll look up, show high one day

Brusque wind burns my heart even now
Brusque wind! I will overfly one day

The world's luxuries follow me on
Love will test me now and try one day

May be those eyes don't roll down any tears
May be the stars and moon defy one day

Neither a home, nor a desire for home now
But the desire may intensify one day

2

Log the jinki aankhon mein andesha koee na tha
Main jis shehr se guzra us me zindaa koee na tha

Cheezon ke ambaar lage the khalq-e Khuda aaraam se thi
Aur mujhe ye ranj wahaan afsurda koee na tha

Hairaani mein hoon aakhir kis ki parchhaaeeen hoon
Wo bhi dhyan mein aaya jis ka saaya koee na tha

Chaunk pada jab yaadon mein us ki aawaaz suni
Bus apni hi goonj thi mujh mein warnaa koee na tha

Main jis khauf mein tha us mein kuchh aur bhi qaidi the
Main jis khwaab mein tha us mein darwaaza koee na tha

2

Such were the people, their eyes showed no sorrow, none
I passed by the city, there was no one alive, none

All around was God's plenty, God's people lived in peace
My only worry: there was no one sad there, none

Whose shadow am I, I don't know, I'm all baffled!
Even he figured in thoughts who had no shadow, none

I was amazed when that voice echoed in memory
That was surely my own voice, no one else's, none

A fear had engulfed me; it had caught others too
I was in a dream and the dream had no exit, none

51

Nida Fazli

Nida Fazli (1938–2016) was born Muqtada Hasan in the city of Delhi, where one of his ancestors had migrated from a place called Fazila in Kashmir. He chose Nida as his pen name and added Fazli after his ancestral home. He received his education in Gwalior, and found his source of livelihood in Bombay as a lyricist. Fazli was a poet, memoirist, and a sensitive commentator on poetry and poets. He earned several awards and gained considerable popularity among both Urdu and Hindi speakers, unlike many of his contemporaries who remained confined to one language.

The most striking feature of Fazli's poetry lies in his ability to exploit the spoken-ness of the spoken word. He drew upon people's language and blended it with the literary traditions of the Sufi-bhakti poets. Rural and urban ladscapes, small hopes and big fears, as well as the loss and retrieval of values, engaged him endlessly. His poetry speaks at a one-to-one level and develops an intimate rapport with the reader, who seems to be close by and listening to the poet intently. Fazli's poetry is dialogic and dramatic in his style of speaking and keeps away from complicated phrasing for his philosophical outpourings. These are amply reflected in his anthologies, memoirs, and even his responses to poetry and poets. *Lafzon Ka Pull, More Naach, Aankh Aur Khwaab Ke Darmiyaan, Safar Mein Dhoop To Hogi, Khoya Hua Sa Kuchh, Mulaaqaatein* and *Deewaron ke Beech* distinguish him for these merits.

I

Insaan mein haiwaan yahaan bhi hai wahaan bhi
Allah nigahbaan yahaan bhi hai wahaan bhi

Khunkhwaar darindon ke faqat naam alag hain
Har shahr bayabaan yahaan bhi hai wahaan bhi

Naaron ka sukoon, waadon ke ghar, khwaabon ki khushiyaan
Baazaar mein saaman yahaan bhi hai wahaan bhi

Ut'thha hai dil-o jaan se dhuaan dono hi jaanib
Ye Mir ka divaan yahaan bhi hai wahaan bhi

I

There is a beast in man—both here and there
While God is so very kind—both here and there

Only the names of bloody beasts differ
All the towns are wild—both here and there

Slogans, promises and happy dreams
All these—market wares—both here and there

Smoke from heart and body on both sides
But Mir's muse is alive—both here and there

2

Brindaaban ke Krishna Kanhaiyyaa Allahu
Bansi, Radha, Geeta, gaiyya Allahu

Thode tinke, thode daane, thoda jal
Aik hi jaisi har gaurayya Allahu

Jaisa jis ka bartan waisa us ka mun
Ghat'ti badh'ti Ganga maiyyaa Allahu

Aik hi darya neela, peela, laal, haraa
Apni apni sab ki naiyya Allahu

Maulwiyon ka sajdaa, pandit ki pooja
Mazdooron ki hayya hayya Allahu

2

Vrindaban's Krishna Kanhaiyya—Allahu
Cows, the flute, Geeta, Radha—Allahu

A few straws, a few grains, and some water
All the sparrows, all alike—Allahu

Just as the owner's ware, so the owner's heart
Falling, rising, Ganga *Maiyya*—Allahu

One stream—blue and yellow, red and green
A boat to each one of them—Allahu

Maulavi's prostratings and pandit's prayers
And the labourer's *haiyya haiyya*—Allahu

52

Irfan Siddiqui

Irfan Siddiqui (1939–2004) was born in Badayun and educated in Bareilly, both towns in Uttar Pradesh. His talent was discovered and celebrated rather late in his literary career. Like Majeed Amjad, he preferred to live a private life and pursue his vocation as a poet and translator in silence and with complete dedication. Siddiqui worked for the Ministry of Information and Broadcasting and kept moving from place to place, and finally chose to settle down in Lucknow where he died, leaving behind a host of admirers, both in India and Pakistan.

Siddiqui can be described as a classicist in the modernist mode—his poetry is a classic site, where the metaphysical and the romantic blend together. Evidently one of the best poets of the contemporary ghazal to reconfigure Persian idiom into Urdu, he engaged with the dichotomies of the perishable-imperishable body and the imperishable-perishable soul. He constructed the dialectics of the physical and the non-physical, the elemental and the mundane, the self and the other—with the help of traditional symbols. He wove a mystical aura of ideas as he dwelt upon the mysteries of the elements, and perceived his material for writing in terms of spirit rather than matter. Siddiqui has left behind six collections—*Canvas, Shab-e Darmiyaan, Saat Samaawaat, Ishq Naama, Hawaa-i Dasht-e Maria* and *Qissa Mukhtasar Karta Hoon.* His complete works are collected in a volume called *Shahr-e Malaal.* Quite in keeping with his interest in things classical, he translated Kalidasa's play, *Malavikagnimitram,* into Urdu, apart from publishing books on the theory of communication.

I

Haq fat'hayaab mere Khuda kyun naheen hua
Too ne kaha tha tera kaha kyun naheen hua

Jab hashr is zameen pe uthhaai gaye to phir
Barpa yaheen pe roz-e jaza kyun naheen hua

Wo shola saaz bhi usee basti ke log the
Un ki gali mein raqs-e hawa kyun naheen hua

Kya jazb-e ishq mujh se ziyaada tha ghair mein
Us ka habeeb us se juda kyun naheen hua

Karta raha main tere liye doston se jung
Too mere dushmanon se khafa kyun naheen hua

Jo kuchch hua kaise hua jaanta hoon main
Jo kuchh naheen hua wo bata kyun naheen hua

I

Why did the right not prevail, my God, why?
You made a promise, your promise failed, why?

Why was the doomsday enacted on this earth, why?
Why was the Day of Judgement not enacted, why?

Those fire mongers too had come from that village
Why did the wind not dance through their lanes, why?

Did he have the spirit of love more than me?
Why wasn't he torn away from his love, why?

I kept on fighting with my friends only for you
Why did you not get angry with my foes, why?

Whatever happened there, I know how that happened
What didn't happen, tell me why that didn't happen, why?

2

Bhool jaaoge ke rahte the yahaan doosre log
Kal phir aabaad karenge ye makaan doosre log

Daf bajaati huee sehraaon se aayegi hawa
Aur phir honge yahaan raqs kunaan doosre log

Inheen maujon pe koee aur jalaaega chiragh
Nazar aainge sar-e aab-e rawaan doosre log

Jal bujhenge ke hum is raat ka indhan hi to hain
Khair, daikhenge naee roshniyaan doosre log

Hum ne ye kaar-e junoon kar to diya hai aaghaaz
Tod daalenge ye zanjeer-e garaan doosre log

Ye bhi gum karda zameenon ki zabaan bolte hain
Apne hi log hain ai hamsafaraan doosre log

Teer chalte rahenge, haath badalte rahenge
Hum giraaein to uthha lenge nishaan doosre log

2

You would soon forget this was the abode for some other people
Tomorrow this abode will home other beings, some other people

Winds from the wilderness will blow in, playing tambourines
  Then this place will get a new herd of some other people

    Some other people shall light new lamps on these waves
    On the water's face will shine bright some other people

    We are the fuel of this night; we shall be put out one day
    The new lights will then show up for some other people

    We have made a move; we have already made a wild move
  Some other day they will break the chains, some other people

    They too speak the language of the lost earth and soil
    They are only us though they look like some other people

  Arrows will be shot, only the shooters shall be some others
    With our fall, our flags will be held up by some other people

53

Kishwar Naheed

Kishwar Naheed (1940–), born in Bulandshahr, Uttar Pradesh, India, migrated to Lahore, Pakistan in 1949, in the wake of India's Partition. Because of severe social constraints, she was compelled to receive her education at home to get a high school diploma through correspondence mode. She mustered her innate courage and studied further to acquire a master's degree in economics from Punjab University, Lahore. She has led a very active life of social and political obligations, apart from attending to her literary commitments. A poet, prose writer, translator, columnist, activist and writer of children's literature, she also held high positions in the government as the editor of the prestigious journal, *Mah-e Nau*, chairperson of the Urdu board, and a part of the Pakistan National Council of the Arts. She also founded *Hawwa*, an organization to aid women to become financially independent through their work in handicrafts and cottage industries.

In literary terms, Naheed may be described best as a fiercely feminist writer, who is concerned especially with impingement of human rights and the politics of citizenship in Pakistan as a newly formed nation state. Her work remains one of the finest examples that illustrate literature as a site of resistance. Through her various kinds of writings, she defined the value of literary text as a testament of courage and faith, which she composed without compromising its aesthetic principles. She is a prolific poet and eight of her poetry collections are put together in a volume titled *Dasht-e Qais Mein Laila*. While she continues to write her poems, her other works have contributed towards the formation of socio-cultural discourse in Pakistan. These books include *Aurat Khwaab Aur Khaak Ke Darmiyaan*, *Buri Aurat Ki Katha*, a biography of Leila Khalid, and the Urdu translation of Simon de Beauvoir's *The Second Sex*.

I

Kuchch din to malaal us ka haq tha
Bichhda to khayaal us ka haq tha

Wo raat bhi din see taazaa rakhta
Shabnam ka jamaal us ka haq tha

Wo tarz-e bayaan mein chaandani tha
Taaron se wisaal us ka haq tha

Tha us ka kharaam mauj-e darya
Lehron ka jalaal us ka haq tha

Baarish ka badan tha us ka hansnaa
Ghunche ka khisaal us ka haq tha

Rakhta tha sambhaal sheesha-i jaan
Tajseem-e kamaal us ka haq tha

Baadal ke misaal us ki khoo thi
Taabeer-e halaal us ka haq tha

Ujlaa tha chambeliyon ke jaisa
Yusuf saa jamaal us ka haq tha

I

My living in grief for a while was only his due
In parting, a thought for him was only his due

He kept his nights as bright as the day but
The beauty of dewdrops was only his due

He was pure moonlight in his eloquence
A while with the stars was only his due

His walk was the majestic move of sea waves
The fury of waves too was only his due

His laughter was a spell of pleasant shower
And the blossom's way was only his due

He treasured his glass-life with great care
Imagining its fineness was only his due

His nature was only like that of the clouds
The moon's dream come alive was only his due

As white as the jasmine blossom was he
Beauty, like Yusuf's, was only his due

2

Dil ko bhi ghum ka saleeqa na tha pehle pehle
Us ko bhi bhoolana achha laga pehle pehle

Dil tha shab zaad use kis se rifaaqat milti
Khwaab taabeer se chhupta raha pehle pehle

Pehle pehle wahi andaaz tha darya jaisa
Paas aa aa ke palat'ta raha pehle pehle

Aankh aaeenon ki hairat naheen jaati ab tak
Hijr ka ghao bhi us ne diya pehle pehle

Khel karne ko bahut the dil-e khwaahish deeda
Kyun hawa dekh jalaaya diya pehle pehle

Umr-e aaindaa ke khwaabon ne pyasa rakhha
Faasla paaon pakadta raha pehle pehle

Naakhun-e bekhabari zakhm banaata hi raha
Koo-e wahshat mein to rasta na tha pehle pehle

Ab to us shakhs ka paikar bhi gul-e khwaab naheen
Jo kabhi mujh mein hee mujh jaisa tha pehle pehle

2

My heart didn't know how to grieve in the early days
He too didn't mind forgetting me in the early days

My heart, a kindred soul of the night, kept the bond
But only the dreams kept shy in the early days

In the early days, it was like the surge of rivers
He came closer; he drew apart in the early days

My mirror-eyes stay amazed even till this day—
How he gave the pangs of parting in the early days

Many a sport for the pining heart to make merry!
Why in the winds I lit a lamp in the early days

My cherished dreams of tomorrow kept me crazy ever
But only the distance checked my feet in the early days

My frenzied nails kept scratching, making wounds
There was no other way in frenzied lanes in the early days

No longer is he the dream-image of a bright blossom
One who lived in me, just like me, in the early days

Ab wo pyasa hai to har boond bhi poochhe nisbat
Wo jo daryaaon pe hansta raha pehle pehle

Wo mulaaqaat ka mausam naheen aaya ab ke
Jo sar-e khwaab sanwarta raha pehle pehle

Ghum ka darya meri aankhon mein simat kar poochhe
Kaun ro ro ke bichhadata raha pehle pehle

Ab jo aankhein hueen sehra to khula har manzar
Dil bhi wahshat ko tarasta raha pehle pehle

Main thi deewar to ab kis ka hai saaya mujh per
Aisa sehra zada chehra na tha pehle pehle

He is thirsty now, now each drop asks him: who are you
He was the one who laughed at the waves in the early days

The season of union did not arrive, this time though
But he adorned himself as a dream in the early days

The river of sorrow flows down my eyes and asks
Who was he that wept at parting in the early days

Now, the eyes are all wilderness, now I can see
How this heart craved to go wild in the early days

I've been a wall ever; whose shadow falls on me today
I didn't have such a bewildered face in the early days

54

Sultan Akhtar

Sultan Akhtar (1940–) was born Sultan Ahmed at his native place, Sahsaram, in Bihar, which is also associated with the Afghan emperor Sher Shah Suri. He received his religious education in a madrasa and earned the degree of Maulavi. Later, he went to school and college but left his graduation studies incomplete, as he went to work at the labour department in the industrial city of Jamshedpur, and then took up a position with the prison department of the government of Bihar. Since his superannuation, he has taken permanent residence in Phulwari Sharif, an ancient centre of Sufi saints and Sufi culture in Patna.

Akhtar came to be recognized for his individual worth as a ghazal writer when the literary magazine *Funoon* (from Lahore) published ten of his compositions in its special issue on the modern Urdu ghazal in 1969. This led to his acceptance in literary circles and subsequent publications of his ghazals in several journals of India and Pakistan in the 1960s. Akhtar earned his identity as a modernist poet without being swayed by the fashionable poetics of the day that considered allusiveness and obscurity as the essential virtues of modernism. Instead, he kept close to the Indo-Persian poetic roots, as he struck a balance between tradition and modernity. His poetry is refined in expression, intimate in tone, and potrays a sympathetic attitude towards life, which he expresses through the metaphors of belonging in a space marked by multiple socio-political crises. His ghazals are collected in *Intesaab, Ghazalistan* and *Pas-e Izhaar-e Hunar*. All these collections, along with his new ghazals, have now appeared in *Sar-e Shaakh-e Talab*.

I

Hum mutma'in hain us ki raza ke baghair bhi
Har kaam chal rahaa hai Khuda ke baghair bhi

Lipti huee hai jism se zanjeer-e maslehat
Be dast-o paa hain log saza ke baghair bhi

Ek kaarobaar-e shauq hi aisa hai jis me ab
Chalta hai kaam makr-o riya ke baghair bhi

Ek lamha apne aap ko yakjaa na kar sake
Hum muntashir hain sail-e bala ke baghair bhi

Ek chup si lag gaee thi mujhe us ke ru-baroo
Main sarnigoon khada tha khata ke baghair bhi

I

I'm so content even without my God's nod
All goes well even without my God's nod

Dubious moves enchain the body, all around
We have lost our limbs even without an assault

It's only the play of passion where all goes well
Even without a trick, even without pretence

I couldn't collect myself even for a moment
I'm so scattered even without a wild wave

I was all stunned, standing face-to-face with Him
I stood with a bowed head even without doing a wrong

2

Wahi besabab benishaan har taraf
Wahi naqsh-e sad raaegaan har taraf

Wahi be iraada safar saamne
Wahi manzilon ka gumaan har taraf

Wahi aag raushan hue khoon mein
Wahi khwahishon ka dhuaan har taraf

Wahi sab ke sab dher hote hue
Wahi tez aandhi rawaan har taraf

Wahi beghari har taraf khemazan
Wahi dher sare makaan har taraf

Wahi waqt ki dhoop dhalti huee
Wahi roze-o shab ka ziyaan har taraf

Wahi jalti bujhti huee zindagi
Wahi koshish-e raaegaan har taraf

Wahi be zarar si zameen chaar soo
Wahi sang dil aasmaan har taraf

2

The same absurd signs showing all around
The same marks of woe growing all around

The same aimless journey staring in the face
The same illusion of goals growing all around

The same fire in the blood glowing all about
The same smoke of desire blowing all around

The same sight—people dropping dead in a row
The same storm in rage blowing all around

The same loss of a home growing all over
The same debris now showing all around

The same sun of time, receding all about
The same days and nights shadowing all around

The same life—bright or blinking all about
The same wasted effort showing all around

The same harmless earth spreading all about
The same unkind sky glowing all around

55

Iftikhar Arif

Iftikhar Arif (1943–), a prominent poet from Pakistan, was born Iftikhar Husain Arif in Lucknow. Before migrating to Pakistan in 1965, he received his education at Madrasa Nizamia in Lucknow and at Lucknow University. In Pakistan, he worked in senior positions at the external services of Pakistan Broadcasting Corporation, Pakistan Television Corporation, Pakistan Scholars and Writers Foundation, Pakistan Academy of Letters, National Language Authority and National Book Foundation. Currently, he is the director general of National Language Promotion Department. He also served as the executive incharge of Urdu Markaz, London and president of Economic Cooperation Organization in Tehran. Arif is a highly respected poet with sixteen awards from national and international bodies, the most prominent among them being Hilal-e Imtiaz, Sitara-i Imtiaz and Pride of Performance from the government of Pakistan.

Arif's poetry constructs myriad conditions of hope and fear,
the essence and prowess of divinity as he experienced it, and
multiple tropes of migration, in a language close to intellectual
ratiocination. His diction is empowered with ironic overtones
which expresses a deep empathy for all those around him.
His poetry harks back to the established Persian poetics and
he revises them to help materialize his own view and vision
of contemporary life as a continuum of times immemorial.
Mehr-e Do Neem, *Harf-e Baaryaab* and *Jahan-e Maloom* are his
collections of poems. His other works include *Shahr-e 'Ilm Ke
Darwaaze Per* and *Kitab-e Dil-o Dunya*.

I

Mere Khuda mujhe itna to m'utabar kar de
Main jis makaan mein rhata hoon us ko ghar kar de

Ye roshni ke ta'aqub mein bhagata hua din
Jo thak gaya hai to ab us ko mukhtasar kar de

Main zindagi ki dua maangne laga hoon bahut
Jo ho sake to duaon ko be asar kar de

Qabeela waar kamaanein khadakne waali hain
Mere lahoo ki gawaahi mujhe nidar kar de

Main apne khwaab se kat kar jiuun to mere Khuda
Ujaad de meri mitti ko dar ba dar kar de

Meri zameen mera akhiri hawaala hai
So main rahoon na rahoon us ko baarawar kar de

I

My God, a real man of me, just make me so
And let my house be my home, just make it so

This day, chasing the light ever without an end
If it's tired, make it shorter, just make it so

I've been praying for a long life, all the while
If you would, return my prayers, just make it so

Tribe by tribe, the swords shall be drawn to rattle now
Let my blood's witness make me brave, just make me so

If I ever live without my cherished dream
Blow out my soil, throw it around, just make me so

My land is the last sign, the last mark, of my being
May I live or die, let it glow, just make it so

2

Mansab na kulaah chahata hoon
Tanha hoon gawaah chahata hoon

Ai ajr-e azeem dene wale
Taufeeq-e gunaah chahata hoon

Darta hoon bahut balandiyon se
Pasti se nibaah chahata hoon

Wo din ke tujhe bhi bhool jaaoon
Us din se panaah chahata hoon

2

Neither a title nor a proud cap do I desire
I'm all alone, only a witness do I require

O the giver of all the bliss and all the pride
Only a small will to sin I must acquire

I am dead scared of heights, truly I am
Now with depths and lows I wish to conspire

May the day I forget you never come
If it does, let me put that day on fire

BEYOND NEW POETICS

Since the 1980s, the Urdu ghazal has shown remarkable variations on the multiple versions of modernism that showed up during the 1950s and after. It is no longer self-conscious as the ghazal of the preceding decades was. The contemporary ghazal has grown out of the modernist need of the previous decades to establish itself as a prominent and individual tradition of literary expression. Transcending the limits of the modernist ghazal, the contemporary ghazal has acquired a certain stability and speaks in much more sober and serious tones. It has been flourishing in both India and Pakistan with greater resilience than before. This newest of the new ghazal has shown infinite passion for life and art; it is perennially positive, as it is against the pensive and the ponderous compositions of the past. Instead of engaging with the problem of identifying themselves as modern or postmodern, today's poets have grown calmer and more composed. They have chosen to engage with the philosophical and mystical aspects of existence and, at the same time, have engaged with history and heritage. Monologic and dialogic in their compositions, the contemporary ghazal addresses the readers as their compatriots and co-readers. These poet-citizens of a larger world have chosen to defy socio-political polarities and speak in a language of common aspirations to compose a literary culture of greater inclusivity and strength. While representing the larger signifiers of a new world order, of new spaces and of new skylines under constant change of colours, contours and schemes, the poets of our times have brought the ghazal to a point of serenity, and from where its future course might be imagined only in terms of possible-impossible turns of future history, and impossible-possible ways of human imagination.

The contemporary ghazal historicizes, politicizes and mythicizes the vital points of contemporary history. It qualifies socio-political cultures on their merits and demerits, interrogates the dichotomies of the modern day-to-day life and living in terms of power-play and broader antinomies in local and global contexts. It chronicles the illusive notions of progress that underline the dynamics of society, economy and polity in the community of competitive nation-states of our times.

56

Sarwat Hussain

Sarwat Hussain (1949–1996), a prominent name among the new wave poets of Pakistan, was born and brought up in Karachi. A college teacher of Urdu by profession, he had the opportunity of drawing upon the great traditions of Urdu poetry and hone a tone of voice and an angle of perception that was essentially his own.

Hussain emerged in the 1970s as a voice to reckon with. Along with his close contemporaries, he contributed towards finding a fresh idiom for the Urdu nazm, where he charged simple prose with a heightened poetical utterance. His ghazal may also be considered alongside his nazm. While engaging with both of these forms, he developed a passionate narrative depicting the sensitive moments of life lived in an age of disillusionment. He is remarkable for his phrasal precision, tonal spark, spontaneity and lucidity. Hussain published the first collection of his poetry titled *Aadhe Sayyaare Per* during his lifetime. Two other collections, *Khaakdaan* and *Aik Katora Paani*, were published posthumously. His collected works have now been published in his *Kulliyaat*.

I

Safeena rakhta hoon darkaar ek samundar hai
Hawaaein kehti hain us paar ek samundar hai

Main ek lehr hoon apne makaan mein aur phir
Hujoom-e koocha-o baazaar ek samundar hai

Ye mera dil hai mera aaeena hai shehzaadi
Aur aaeene mein giraftaar ek samundar hai

Kahaan wo pairahan-e surkh aur kahaan wo badan
Ke aks-e maah se bedaar ek samundar hai

Ye intehaa-i musarrat ka shahr hai Sarwat
Yahaan to har dar-o deewaar ek samundar hai

I

I have a vessel with me, I need a sea
The breeze tells me at that end there lies a sea

I'm a wave in my abode and beyond all that
The swarm at the souks and the streets is but only a sea

Princess! This is my heart, this my mirror
And in the mirror, lies imprisoned a sea

That bloodshot garment here, there a glowing body
Alive with the moon's reflection, there lies a sea

This is the city of infinite joy, Sarwat
Here, each door, each wall, is but a sea

2

Achha sa koee sapna dekho aur mujhe dekho
Jaago to aaeena dekho aur mujhe dekho

Socho ye khaamosh musaafir kyun afsurda hai
Jab bhi tum darwaaza dekho aur mujhe dekho

Sub'ha ke farsh pe goonja us ka aik sukhan
Kirnon ka guldasta dekho aur mujhe dekho

Baazoo hain ya do patwaarein naao pe rakhhi hain
Lehrein leta draya dekho aur mujhe dekho

Do hi cheezein is dunya mein dekhne waali hain
Mitti ki sundarta dekho aur mujhe dekho

2

Have a dream, a good one, and look at me
When awake, look at the mirror, look at me

Think, why this silent voyager is so sad
When you look at the door, look at me

On the dawn's floor echoed her sole voice
Look at the urn of rays, look at me

These are arms, or two oars on the boat
Look at the surging river, look at me

Only two things in this world are there to see
Look at the soil's wondrous beauty, look at me

57

Farhat Ehsas

Farhat Ehsas (1950–) was born Farhatullah Khan in Bahraich, Uttar Pradesh, India. He received his early education in Bahraich, and then joined Lucknow University for a short period of time. He got his master's degrees in English Literature and Islamic Studies from Jamia Millia Islamia, New Delhi, and Aligarh Muslim University, Aligarh, respectively. He worked as a freelance journalist before joining the Urdu daily, *Qaumi Awaz*, in New Delhi. He has also been associated with the editing of *Islam and the Modern Age* and *Islam Aur Asr-e Jadeed*, published by Jamia Millia Islamia. He has written extensively on society, culture, politics and literature for the Urdu Press and the All India Radio, apart from producing scripts for documentaries and TV serials. He works as the chief of editorial department at Rekhta Foundation.

One of the most remarkable poets among his contemporaries, Ehsas writes poetry rich with metaphors in a language that is accessible and a style that is liberated from all constraints of the poetic and the non-poetic. His apprehensions are characteristically mystical and his references essentially philosophical. He views his content with detachment and renders them universal without being heavily allusive and obscure. His collections, *Main Rona Chahataa Hoon* and *Shairi Naheen Hai Yeh*, have been received well and have made way for more remarkable work in the future. *Qashqa Khaincha Dair Mein Baithha* is a comprehensive collection of his works in the Devanagiri script.

I

Ye baagh zinda rahe ye bahaar zinda rahe
Main mar bhi jaaoon to kya mera yaar zinda rahe

Qadeem raaste rooposh hote jaate hain
So tera koocha teri rahguzaar zinda rahe

Hamesha saaz bajaati rahe yun hi teri zulf
Aur us ke saaz ka ek ek taar zinda rahe

Ye khaak zinda inheen aansuon ke dam se hai
Har ek deeda-i aansoo sh'aar zinda rahe

Faraar rooh huee saara naqd-e jaan le kar
Hum apne jism se le kar udhaar zinda rahe

Main tere ghar yoon hi be-qaid aata jaata rahoon
Teri nazar mein mera aitebaar zinda rahe

Hazaar shukria Ehsas ji un aankhon ka
Hum un ke teer ka ho kar shikaar zinda rahe

I

May this garden live long, may this spring live long
It doesn't matter if I die, may my friend live long

Old paths go into hiding with each passing day
May your lane live long, may your street live long

May your tresses play their music all along
May the music play long, may the strings live long

This earth lives on for the tears shed here
May each tear's nursing glance, live on, live long

The soul flew away claiming all the cost of life
Drawing on a loan from the body, we did live long

May I keep coming to your place without a check
May your eyes hold me in trust, may your trust live long

Many thanks, Ehsas-ji, to those obliging looks
I sustained all its arrows and I lived long

2

Tujhe khabar ho to bole ai mere sitaara-i shab
Meri samjh mein to aataa naheen ishaara-i shab

Use main aik musalsal chiraagh kar deta
Meri giraft mein hota jo ista'ara-i shab

Main ek chiraagh kahaan tak muzaahimat karta
Mere khilaaf tha kitna bada idaara-i-shab

Bahut se chaand bahut se chiraagh kam nikle
Banaane baithha jo main raat goshwara-i shab

Kisi bhi sub'ha ka marham asar naheen karta
Ke har sehar hai yahaan doosra kinaara-i shab

2

If you know, let me know too, my dear stars of night
I just can't make out the signs of the stars of night

I would have turned it into a lamp burning in rows
If I could lay my hand on the metaphor of night

I was a lonely lamp; how could I ever resist
There stood in front the colossal designs of night

Many a moon, many a lamp, but they proved less
When I sat to account for an account of night

No dawns can ever bring a soothing touch to me
Every dawn is but only another end of night

58

Ashufta Changezi

Ashufta Changezi (1951–?) was born in Bareilly, where he received his early education. He acquired a BA (Honours) degree from Aligarh Muslim University, Aligarh. He worked in the Post and Telegraph department for his living, before moving to Saudi Arabia to better his professional prospects. He disappeared in 1996 and has not been heard of ever since.

Changezi was a poet of rare sensitivities. His poetry is one of an intimate dialogue with his own self. He reflected upon the mysterious relationship between nature and man, as well as upon the inter-relationship between man and man to develop a narrative of power and powerlessness. His poetry is especially successful in its abundant depiction of natural and nature-related images, showing them in their resplendence, but also always in relation to the human predicament. His collection of ghazals, *Shikaston ki Fasl*, *Gard Baad* and *Shehr-e Gumaan*, stand out for these qualities he represented with distinction.

I

Ye bhi naheen beemaar na the
Itne junoon aasaar na the

Logon ka kya zikr karein
Hum bhi kam 'ayyaar na the

Ghar mein aur bahut kuchh tha
Sirf dar-o deewaar na the

Sab per hansna shewa tha
Jab tak khud us paar na the

Teri khabar mil jaati thee
Shahr mein jab akhbaar na the

Pehle bhi sab kuchh bikta tha
Khwabaon ke baazaar na the

Maut ki baatein pyari theen
Marne ko tayyaar na the

I

Not that I was never riled
But never so very wild

Not to talk of the people
I was no less profiled

There was enough at home too
Not only walls and doors piled

Making fun, a dear habit
Only till I wasn't beguiled

I got to get your news when
The city was not so filed

Then also, all could be bought
But no market with dreams piled

We were enamoured, talking of death
But with dying not reconciled

2

Aankhein hain chakaachaund pa jhilmil to likhunga
Main tera saraapa na sahi til to likhunga

Kya shart lagaa dee ke tera zikr na aai
Lekin kaheen dushman kaheen qaatil to likhunga

Ye such hai isee shahr ka baashinda hoon main bhi
Naghma na sahi shor-e salaasil to likhunga

Samjhe jo koee kaar-e junoon us ko samajh le
Naam apna kabhi tere muqaabil to likhunga

Yoon dekho to sahil bhi samundar se laga hai
Saahil jise samjha use saahil to likhunga

Qarz aur bhi kitnon ke hain Ashufta chukaane
Har haal mein phir bhi use shaamil to likhunga

2

The eyes are ablaze but in a haze I must write
That I'm not your image but about your mole I must write

What a condition that you may not be mentioned!
But now an enemy, now an assassin I must write

It is true; I too am one from this very city
If not music, the clank of chains I must write

Whosoever thinks it wild, is free to think
My name, just opposite yours I must write

At a distance, the shore too looks next to the sea
That I thought a shore was a shore I must write

Many a debt I need to pay off Ashufta
On all occasions, he stood by I must write

59

Jamal Ehsani

Jamal Ehsani (1951–1998) was born in Sargodha, Pakistan. He received his early education there and then shifted to Karachi. He was a self-proclaimed bohemian, ever defying a sense of arrival. Impatient with a principled life as it suffocated him, he yearned for freedom under open skies and associated his freedom as being one with the world of elements. His poetry appealed to the younger generation as they could identify themselves with him because he wrote of their aspirations.

Ehsani's poetry is richly melancholic. Even though he constructed the conditions of deprivation with metaphoric precision, he looked at life with hope and faith. He indulged in the act of negotiating with life in simple and plain terms now, now in philosophically complex manners. He concretized the ambiguities of existence and the human power of perseverance in a refreshingly new vocabulary that also showed his understanding of the classical poetic language and the possibility of revisioning it. He exploited this potential to project his understanding of life's manifestations, which in turn, are represented in his collections. These are noticeable in his collections that include *Sitaara-i Safar*, *Raat Ke Jaage Hue* and *Taare Ko Mehtab Kiya*. They were finally put together in the volume titled *Kulliyaat-e Jamal*.

I

Hamraah tere mansab-o lashkar zuroor hai
Lekin shikast tera muqaddar zuroor hai

Gardish mein aaj mere sitare hain gar to kya
Tera bhi aik waqt muqarrar zuroor hai

Kya hai, ye mujh ko 'ilm naheen ho saka abhi
Kuchh hai ke jo bisaat se baahar zuroor hai

Rehtaa yun hi naheen hai tah-o baala ye nizaam
Is kaaenaat mein koee chakkar zuroor hai

Ye hukm hai ke koee banaai na kashtiyaan
Is shahr ke kinaare samundar zuroor hai

Qadr-e dil-e mahaajir-e khasta karo ke ye
Be shajra-i nasab naheen beghar zuroor hai

Shaayad samajh gaya wo dar-o bast-e khaana se
Is ghar mein koee doosra bistar zuroor hai

I

You enjoy all the power, all the glory, I'm sure
But defeat, surely defeat is your share, I'm sure

It doesn't matter if my stars don't favour me
Your days too are counted, that's for sure, I'm sure

I could not ever find what the matter was
But something lies beyond my control, I'm sure

The earth is not shattered without reason
There must be something quite strange, I'm sure

Let none make a boat—that's a command for all
Surely, a sea hides by city's shore, I'm sure

Respect the poor migrant, respect his heart and soul
He's homeless but has a lineage to show, I'm sure

The way the house is kept, he has come to guess
Surely, someone else lives here now, I'm sure

2

Tark-e baada hai aur lambi raat
Aab-e saada hai aur lambi raat

Meri aankhein hain aur diyon ki qataar
Tera waada hai aur lambi raat

Odh kar so raha hoon khaali jaam
Kam libaada hai aur lambi raat

Gul hua maikade ka sadr chiraagh
gham ziyaada hai aur lambi raat

Sub'ha dam wo dikhaayi de ke na de
Ek iraada hai aur lambi raat

Ek mahal ki ghulaam gardishon mein
Shaahzaada hai aur lambi raat

Aaj gaur-e kabirul aulia per
Peerzaada hai aur lambi raat

2

This vow of abstinence and this long night
Plain water for a drink and this long night

Here, my eyes and there, a row of lamps
Thoughts of your promise and this long night

The cup is empty, I live with this cup
Not much to live by and this long night

The prime lamp of the tavern is put out
So much to grieve on and this long night

She may show up the next morning, she may not
To live with a flaming desire and this long night

In the waiting lounge of a grand palace
A prince in waiting and this long night

On the tomb of a master saint tonight
The tomb-keeper alone and this long night

60

Perveen Shakir

Perveen Shakir (1952–1994) was born in Karachi, Pakistan. She acquired two master's degrees in English Literature and English Linguistics from the University of Karachi, in 1972 and 1980 respectively. Following this, she received a Fulbright Scholar-in-Residence Teaching Scholarship at the University of Hartford, USA in 1990, and a master's degree in Public Administration from the John F. Kennedy School of Government, Harvard (USA) in 1992. She also did a six-week Management Information System course from Lahore University. Shakir joined as an English faculty in 1973, before joining the Pakistani civil services to work in a number of important positions. She had a long list of eighteen certificates and awards to her credit, in recognition of her talent as a poet, academic and administrator. She also received five awards posthumously. Her distinguished career came to an end when her car met with an accident in Islamabad, from which she could not survive.

Shakir was essentially a poet of romantic disposition. She wrote of aspirations and despair. She spoke in a personal voice without assuming a persona which imparted an immediacy of appeal to her poetry. She was also concerned with social dichotomies, taboos, gender issues and other social discriminations. All these are reflected in her work with equal honesty. Her collections include *Khushboo*, *Sadbarg*, *Khudkalaami* and *Inkaar*, which were collected together in *Maah-e Tamaam* during her lifetime. Her last book of poems, *Kaf-e Aaeena*, was published posthumously. Her newspaper columns were put together in *Gosha-i Chashm*.

I

Poora dukh aur aadha chaand
Hijr ki shab aur aisa chaand

Din mein wahshat bahal gaee thi
Raat huee aur nikla chaand

Kis maqtal se guzra hoga
Itna sehma sehma chaand

Yadon ki aabad gali mein
Ghoom raha hai tanha chaand

Mere karwat pe jaag uthhe
Neend ka kitnaa kachcha chaand

Mere munh ko kis hairat se
Dekh raha hai bhola chaand

Itne ghane baadal ke peechhe
Kitna tanha hoga chaand

Aansoo roke noor nahaai
Dil darya tun sehra chaand

Itne raushan chehre per bhi
Sooraj ka hai saaya chaand

Jub paani mein chehra dekha
Tu ne kis ko socha chaand

I

My pain is full but only half the moon
Such a night of parting and such a moon!

My madness was much tamed in daytime
But when the night came appeared the moon

Which ghastly gallows it must have passed by
This moon, such a scared, nervous moon

In the lanes, alive with blissful memories
Wanders alone a cheerless, gloomy moon

It wakes up when I turn from side to side
So very light of sleep, the delicate moon

How astonishing! How it looks at me!
That innocent one, that childish moon

Behind such thick and dark clouds
How lonely would be the moon

Holding tears, washed in beams of light
Heart—a brook, a body—a desert-moon

Even on such a glowing, radiant face
Only a shadow of the sun—the moon

When you saw your face in clear water
Tell me truly who did you think of, moon?

2

Tera ghar aur mera jungle bheegata hai saath saath
Aisi barsatein ke baadal bheegata hai saath saath

Bachpane ka saath hai, phir aik sé dono ke dukh
Raat ka aur mera aanchal bheegata hai saath saath

Wo ajab dunya ke sub khanjar bakaf phirte hain aur
Kaanch ke pyalon mein sandal bheegata hai saath saath

Barish-e sang-e malaamat mein bhi wo hamraah hai
Main bhi bheegoon khud bhi paagal bheegata hai saath saath

Ladkiyon ke dukh ajab hote hian, such us se ajeeb
Hans rahi hain aur kaajal bheegata hai saath saath

Barishein jaade ki aur tanha bahut mera kisaan
Jism aur eklauta kambal bheegata hai saath saath

2

Both your home and my jungle get wet together
Such heavy rains, all the clouds get wet together

They are the cohorts of childhood; their pains are the same
The scarves of night and that of mine get wet together

What a bizarre world! There they move with daggers in hand
In the glass bowls, the sandalwoods get wet together

He was with me no matter what curse, what blight
I get wet, that crazy one too gets wet together

The pains of girls are strange; their truths stranger
Both their chuckles and their kohl get wet together

The winter rains and the poor peasant all alone
His lonely body and only blanket get wet together

61

Ishrat Afreen

Ishrat Afreen (1956–) was named Ishrat Jehan at her birth in Karachi, Pakistan. She studied there and acquired her BA and MA degrees in Urdu Literature. She started her professional career as an assistant editor of *Aawaaz* (Karachi), then edited by the eminent poet, Fehmida Riaz. Her poetry was featured on Radio Pakistan. She shifted to India after her marriage and later went to the United States of America, where she remained associated with teaching at the University of Texas, Austin, in its Hindi–Urdu Flagship Programme. Later, she moved to Karachi.

Afreen is one of those prominent poets whose work engages with the issues of women in Pakistan. Her poetry draws upon a private hinterland of the local flora and fauna with which she identified intimately and which included simple folks, open fields, food grains, the blowing wind and a kind earth. She also wrote of her diasporic longings for a home left behind. Her vocabulary is distinct and her turns of phrase spell out her affiliations to her personal and political space. Afreen has two collections to her credit—*Kunj Peele Phuloon Kaa* and *Dhoop Apne Hisse Ki*.

I

Ladkiyaan maaon jaise muqaddar kyun rakhti hain
Tan sehra aur aankh samundar kyun rakhti hain

Auratein apne dukh ki wiraasat kis ko dengi
Sandooqon mein bund ye zewar kyun rakhti hain

Wo jo aap hi pooji jaane key laayaq theen
Champa si poron mein pathhar kyun rakhti hain

Wo jo rahi hain khaali pet aur nange paaon
Bacha bacha ker ser ki chaadar kyun rakhti hain

Band haveli mein jo saanahe ho jaate hain
Un ki khabar deewarein aksar kyun rakhti hain

Subh-e-wisaal ki kirnein hum se poochh rahi hain
Raatein apne haath mein khanjar kyun rakhti hain

I

Why do the girls share their fates with their mothers, why?
Why are their bodies all wilderness, eyes all ocean, why?

Who would these women make the lasting heirs of
their pain?
Why do they keep gems and jewels hidden in a vault, why?

Once, they were the ones fit to be revered but now
Why do they keep pebbles in *champa* limbs, why?

They survived empty stomach, bare feet but now
Why do these women save their head-covers, why?

Dark plots often thicken in the well-guarded palaces
Why do the walls keep secrets in their chests, why?

The first rays of the dawn of union ask me now:
Why do the nights keep swords in their hands, why?

2

Jinhein ki 'umr bhar suhaag ki duaaein dee gaeen
Suna hai apni choodiyaan hi pees kar wo pee gaeen

Bahut hai ye rawaayaton ka zahr saari 'umr ko
Jo talkhiyaan hamaare aanchalon mein baandh dee gaeen

Kabhi na aisi fasl mere gaaon mein hui ke jab
Kusum ke badle chunriyaan gulaab se rangee gaeen

Wo jin ke pairahan ki khushbuein hawa pe qarz theen
Ruton ki wo udaas shaahzaadiyaan chali gaeen

Un ungliyon ko choomana bhi bid'atein shumaar hon
Wo jin ke khaakh per numoo ki aayatein likhi gaeen

Saron ka ye lagaan ab ke fasl kaun le gaya
Ye kis ki khetiyaan thheen, kis ko saunp dee gaeen

2

All prayers for their happy union for all life
But also a drink of crushed bangles for all life

Enough, this curse of customs for all life
Enough bitterness tied to our robes for all life

We never had such a crop in our village, never
Not safflower but roses dyed our scarves for all life

The breeze owed us the fragrance of her robes but
The sad princess of seasons vanished for all life

How can the kissing of those fingers look strange
On whose soil the songs of life were written for all life

Who robbed us of the toll of heads this season?
Whose crops were these, who got them all for all life?

62

Asad Badayuni

Asad Badayuni (1958–2003) was born Asad Ahmed in Badayun, Uttar Pradesh. Following the tradition of the past poets, he chose to append the name of his native place to his own name, as it was of great historical, cultural and literary significance to him. He received his early education in his hometown and worked at Aligarh Muslim University as an Urdu professor. He died there, following an illness.

Badayuni is a prominent voice among his contemporaries. He dwelt upon finite nature of life as well as the infinite nature of time, and sought his metaphors in the timelessness of history and the imperishability of cultural heritage. He developed his own mythologies to interpret time and space by annotating the prevalent meaning of pain and duplicity, dreams and despair, reality and fantasy. Strong visual and auditory imagination characterize his poetry. Badayuni published six collections of his poetry, namely, *Gul-e Rangeen, Dhoop ki Sarhad, Khema-i Khwaab, Junoon Kinaara, Daastaani Ghazlein* and *Wara-i Sher*. These were collected in his *Kulliyaat* posthumously. He also published five books of literary criticism.

I

Zameen se khalaa ki taraf jaaunga
Wahaan se Khuda ki taraf jaaunga

Bukhara-o Baghdad-o Basra ke baad
Kisee karbalaa ki taraf jaaunga

Chaman se bulaawaa bahut hai magar
Main dasht-e balaa ki taraf jaaunga

Chamakta damakta nagar chhod kar
Phir us bewafaa ki taraf jaaunga

Rifaaqat ki raahon mein kuchh bhi naheen
Yahaan se jafaa ki taraf jaaunga

Badan ka muqaddar hai laahasilee
Main zehn-e rasaa ki taraf jaaunga

Agar main na aaghaaz mein mar gayaa
To phir intihaa ki taraf jaaunga

Chiraagh aarzoo ke jalaa kar kaee
Safeer-e hawaa ki taraf jaaunga

I

From the earth to space, I will set off
Then for God's land of grace, I will set off

Past Bukhara, Baghdad and Samarkand
For a Karbala's space, I will set off

Although the gardens beckon me much
For the country of disgrace, I will set off

Leaving behind the shining, gleaming towns
For my faithless love's embrace, I will set off

Love has nothing to offer, nothing at all
Not to write love but to efface, I will set off

The body is set to dissolve in a void
For thought's grandeur and grace, I will set off

If I don't perish at the start itself
For the very last trace, I will set off

I will burn many a lamp of longing
Then for the wind's base, I will set off

2

Meri ruswaayi ke asbaab hain mere ander
Aadmi hoon so bahut khwaab hain mere ander

Mere baahar nazar aaigi tujhe khaak hi khaak
Kaee jugnu kaee mehtaab hain mere ander

Wo bahaarein jo sar-e sat'h-e zameen khatm hueen
Dekh le aaj bhi shaadaab hain mere ander

Mujh ko sehra na samajh aur mere zaahir pe na ja
Kaee darya kaee taalaab hain mere ander

Maikade tak mujhe jaane ki zuroorat kya hai
Humnashinaan-e ma-i-naab hain mere ander

Mujh ko marne se bachaa to naheen sakte jaanaan
Zinda rahne ke jo asbaab hain mere ander

Sair kar too bhi ye majmoo'a pareshaani ka
Mujh se bichhde hue ahbaab hain mere ander

2

The reasons for my disgrace lie within me
I'm human, many a dream fly within me

Beyond me, it is all dust and ash, all around
Many a moon, many a firefly within me

Springs that perished from the face of this earth
Are all aglow in a sky within me

I'm no wilderness; don't go by my looks alone
Many ponds and many streams ply within me

Why go to the tavern if my kindred kin
Drunk on pure wine are so high within me

You can't save me from dying, you can't, my love
Reasons to survive multiply within me

You too should pass through this fare of miseries
All dear, departed friends lie within me

63

Khursheed Akbar

Khursheed Akbar (1959–), who was named Mohammad Khursheed Alam, was born at Barbigha in Munger, Bihar. He acquired two master's degrees in Political Science and in Urdu. Currently, Akbar is a senior member of the Bihar administrative service and lives in Patna.

Akbar carved a way for himself away from both the Progressive and the modernist poets. Sensitive perceptions of the physical and the spiritual, here and now, of the individual and the society clearly mark his poetry. He found space in his ghazals to reflect upon the alternating despairs and bliss of contemporary life. He appropriated ordinary speech to his purpose and charged it with greater vitality. Even while he respected the past traditions of writing, he tried to achieve a distance from them to arrive at a voice and a style that was distinctly his own. His collections of poems include *Samundar*

Khilaaf Rehta Hai, Badan Kashti Bhanwar Khwahish and *Falak Pehloo Mein.* He has a critical study titled *Aik Bhasha, Do Likhaawat, Do Adab: Aik Tanqueedi Jaayeza* to his credit. Akbar is also the honorary editor of the literary journal, *Aamad.*

I

Lakeeron se bandhi taqdeer gum sum
Hatheli ki har ek tadbeer gum sum

Faseel-e shahr per aayat luhoo ki
Quran-e dard ki tafseer gum sum

Kunware khwab ne odhee zaeefi
Hai aaeenon mein kyun hamsheer gum sum

Khanakte qahqahon ki bebasi per
Mere kamre mein ek tasweer gum sum

Ragon mein kaisi kaisi khalbali hai
Mere pehloo mein hai shamsheer gum sum

mezaajon mein wahi darbaar daari
Tapakti raal mein jageer gum sum

Dilon ki masjid-e wiraan mein Akbar
Azaan khaamosh hai takbeer gum sum

I

A fate tied to the lines of fate, lost
Every endeavour of the hand, lost

Verses in blood on the city's frontiers
The meaning of pain's testament, lost

The bachelor dreams have grown old now
Why in the mirror, the sister lost

On the helplessness of loud laughter
A photograph in my room looks lost

What a hubbub in the humming veins
By my own side, my own sword lost

In nature, just the same surrender
In temptation, all inheritance lost

In the deserted mosque of hearts, Akbar
Call for prayer silent, verse of prayer lost

2

Hukmaraani bayaan se baahar hai
Bebasee ab makaan se baahar hai

Dard ka zaaeqa bataoon kya
Ye 'ilaaqa zabaan se baahar hai

Wo Madeena hai main mohajir hoon
Ye ta'alluq gumaan se baahar hai

Ek sajda hai apni marzi ka
Wo tere aastaan se baahar hai

Dhoop chaahe shadeed ho jitni
Aap ke saibaan se baahar hai

Aik muthhi zameen ki khwahish bhi
Sarhad-e aasmaan se baahar hai

Aakhri aadmi qabeele ka
Dekh, shahr-e amaan se baahar hai

Ek patta hai shaakh-e 'uryaan per
Jo muraad-e khazaan se baahar hai

Kaun Khursheed ko kahe apna
Wo to dono jahaan se baahar hai

2

Power play goes beyond description
Helplessness wanders beyond a home

How to describe the taste of pain
The taste is now beyond the tongue

He is Medina; I, a migrant
This bond is beyond conjecture

I bow down, but only as I wish
My bowing is beyond your threshold

Howsoever hot be the sun
It burns beyond your canopy

A desire for a handful of the earth
Lies beyond the reach of the sky

The very last man of the tribe
Stays beyond the city of mercy

A leaf sits on a naked branch
That's beyond the desire of autumn

None would consider Khursheed his own
He stays beyond both the worlds

64

Zeeshan Sahil

Zeeshan Sahil, (1961–2008) was born in Hyderabad, Sind. He received his education there and in Karachi, where he lived a rather short life of forty-seven years, owing to physical deformity and illness. He worked as a columnist for Pakistan Broadcasting Corporation and briefly remained associated with the National Book Council of Pakistan.

Sahil was a poet of remarkable resilience in terms of his experiential capital and its unassuming rendition. He held a prominent place among the postmodernist poets of Pakistan. Drawing upon a broader realm of experiences, he evolved a kind of diction that could explore the socio-political conditions of his times in both allusive and direct terms. This enabled him to depict sundry images and make statements that were direct and precise in spite of being referential. Sahil formulated a unique discourse in his poetry as he authenticated the prose poem and moved from the mundane to the reflective. His collections, *Arena, Chidiyon Ka Shore, Kuhr Aalood Aasman Ke Sitare, Karachi Aur Doosri Nazmein, Shabnaama Aur Doosri Nazmein,* and *Email Aur Doosri Nazmein, Jung Ke Dinon Mein* and *Neem Tareek Mohabbat* bear testimony to the vitality of his all-inclusive imagination.

I

Yaad karne ke zamaane se bahut aage hain
Aaj hum apne thikaane se bahut aage hain

Koee aa kar hamein dhoondega to kho jaaega
Hum naye gham mein puraane se bahut aage hain

Jism baaqi hai magar jaan ko mitaane waale
Rooh mein zakhm nishaane se bahut aage hain

Is qadar khush hain ke hum khwab-e-faraamoshi mein
Jaag jaane ke bahaane se bahut aage hain

Jo hamein paa ke bhi khone se bahut peechhe tha
Hum use kho ke bhi paane se bahut aage hain

I

I am far beyond the age of recalling
Far beyond my abode today, far beyond

Whosoever comes to look for me will now get lost
In new sorrows, I'm far beyond the old ones, far beyond

The body lives on but the plunderers of my soul should know
Wounds in the soul are far beyond the targets, far beyond

Happy, I'm so happy, in the dreams of forgetfulness
I'm far beyond the pleas of waking up, far beyond

One who was far behind in losing even in finding me
In losing her, I'm far beyond in finding, far beyond

2

Yoon boli thi chidiya khaali kamre mein
Jaise koee naheen tha khaali kamre mein

Har pal mera rasta dekha karta hai
Jaane kis ka saaya khaali kamre mein

Khidki ke raste se laaya karta hoon
Main baahar ki dunya khaali kamre mein

Har mausam mein aate jaate rehte hain
Log hawa aur darya khaali kamre mein

Chehron ke jungle se lekar aaya hoon
Surkh gulaab ka pauda khaali kamre mein

Basti mein har raat nikalne waala chaand
'Umr hui na utra khaali kamre mein

Tez hawaa mein saare kooze toot gaye
Aur phaila ek sehra khaali kamre mein

Sahil shahr se door akela rehta hai
Jaise main hoon rehta khaali kamre mein

2

So spoke a bird in the empty room
As if there was none in the empty room

I wonder whose shadow in the empty room
Waits for me, every moment, in the empty room

I bring inside the world spread outside
Through my window in the empty room

They keep coming, going, every season
People, wind, river, in the empty room

I have brought in from the jungle of faces
A plant of red roses in the empty room

That moon showing up in the village every night
Ages now, it hasn't shown up in the empty room

Earthen pots broke to pieces in the howling wind
Then spread a wilderness in the empty room

The shore lives all alone, far from the city
As I live all alone in the empty room

65

Aftab Husain

Aftab Husain (1962–) is a Pakistan-born and Austria-based poet who writes in both Urdu and English. He completed his doctorate in comparative literature from the University of Vienna, Austria, where he currently teaches courses on south Asian literature and culture. He has two collections of poetry in English—both were published in Vienna along with their German translations. His poems have been translated into French, Italian, Serbian, Arabic and Persian. He himself translates German poetry into Urdu and vice versa. Aftab Husain co-edits a German/English bilingual magazine *Words & World,* that highlights migrant literature from Vienna, Austria and writes in Pakistani–English newspapers on the issues of literary culture.

Aftab Husain writes metric and non-metric poems as well as ghazals. To his Urdu readers, however, he is distinguished for his ghazals that have received critical as well as popular acclaim. His ghazals are marked by a certain waywardness of thought and an offbeat twist of inferences that he manages to control with his mastery over language. His lines, although almost prosaic in syntax, are chiselled in the precision of their euphonic diction. Writing across a wide thematic spectrum, the poetry of Aftab Husain leaves a lot unsaid, which renders to his ghazals a poly-vocal postmodern significance. He has published one collection of his poems titled *Matla*.

I

Jidhar nigaah karoon ek naya samundar hai
Ye khwaab hai ke koee khwaab ka samundar hai

Nazar uthhaaoon to haibat se kaanp jaata hoon
Wo husn hai ke bipharta hua samundar hai

Main us ko aankh mein bhar loon ke us mein doob maroon
Ye mere saamne gehra khula samundar hai

Bahaa ke le gaee raat us ki baat baat mujhe
So main hoon aur koee goonjta samundar hai

Wo yaad dil mein dar aai hai aur khula mujh per
Samundaron se ulajhti hawa samundar hai

Jo paar utarna hi thehra to koee farq naheen
Ke meri raah mein dunya hai yaa samundar hai

I

Wherever I see, I see a new sea
Is that a sea of dreams, or a dream of a sea

When I look up, I just shudder with fright
Is that a beauty, or a fuming sea

Shall I preserve her in my eyes, or perish in her
There lies before me a deep, an open sea

Each act of hers sailed me afar last night
So this is me, that a resounding sea

With her memory in my heart, I know now
The wind confronting the sea is but a sea

I've to sail through and arrive; doesn't matter
What lies on my way—the world, or the sea

2

Rok sakta tha kisee ko main magar jaane diya
Mujh mein koee mar raha tha main magar jaane diya

Khwaab tha aankhon mein meri, main ne aankhein khol deen
Aur us khushboo ko saare mein bikhar jaane diya

Rafta rafa dil ko dunya ki hawaa raas aa gaee
Rafta rafta hum ne apna zakhm bhar jaane diya

Aur ab wo log meri raah ki deewaar hain
Jin ko main ne apne ander se guzar jaane diya

Shaam koee dil se ho kar jaa raha tha Aftab
Hum ne dekha ek nazar aur dekh kar jaane diya

2

I could have stopped someone, I let that someone go
Someone was dying in me, I let that someone die

There was a dream in my eyes, I just opened my eyes
And that fragrance around, I let the fragrance spread

Only by and by, my heart got used to the world's ways
And only by and by, I also let my wounds heal

And now they—only they stand like walls in my way
For whom I made a way through my heart, I let them go

Last evening someone passed through the alleys of my heart
I saw that someone, Aftab, I let that someone leave

TRANSLATOR'S NOTE

Urdu and the Ghazal

The Urdu ghazal is a major repository of cultural signifiers usually and largely associated with Muslims in India. Over a period of more than five centuries, it has grown and developed across the country as the most popular poetic form. Justifiably, the history of this quintessential form of poetry is also the history of the development of Urdu as a language of literary expression. In spite of the frequent debates regarding the lack of patronage to this language, its unsteady survival in its own habitats, and the linguistic mapping of more or less viable languages, the Urdu language has retained its place in the socio-cultural matrix of India, precisely because the ghazal has stood it in good stead and has ensured it a life along with other languages of India. Hence, there is a need to put this remarkable tradition of the Urdu ghazal across a larger readership in the English language for all its veracity and variety.

This Collection

I have tried to put together a comprehensive collection of Urdu ghazals from its very beginnings in the late sixteenth century to the present times. I have identified seven literary periods and selected sixty-five poets to create a historical perspective and to show the development of this poetic form, in both India and Pakistan. A detailed account of the pretext, text, and context of the ghazal in general, and the Urdu ghazal in particular, is presented at the beginning to create a larger perspective on the form. This is followed by a critical introduction to each period and the selected poets who made their mark and stayed on to be a part of the larger canon. All these are supplementary efforts to make way for the reader to reach the ghazals in English translation. This collection aspires to serve as a point of reference to mark the best ghazals written through ages, and also to show how the ghazal stands out as a literary form to which there is no other approximate form in any other language.

Methodology of Translation

Translating the ghazal has been a different kind of experience for me, compared with my earlier experience of translating the Urdu nazm, or the regular poem. It has been a matter of approximating a form and meeting the attendant demands that it made in the process. As such, I have tried to retain the formal structure of the ghazal comprising a set of *shers*. Considering the ghazal as a macrocosm and the *sher* as a microcosm, I have tried to retain the remarkable precision of each *sher* by finding space for all the units of ideas by evolving a pattern of punctuation which is sometimes in contravention of the standard practice of punctuation. I have done this to ease the tension of ideas and also to control the line length which, in turn, is regulated, as far as possible, by a uniform number of syllables used in a line. This is further modulated by words of similar length in most cases. I have practised this to help the reader appreciate the precision of each couplet and also to help him apprehend the internal rhythm of the composition. Much that I have tried to do is, to a considerable extent, conditioned by the need to create a design of possible meaning in a structure of rhythm and end rhymes which characterizes the ghazal as a poetic composition.

An End Note

It must also be mentioned at the end that the idea and the experience of 'love' in the ghazal tradition is based on a liberal understanding of life, both in romantic and divine terms. This implies that the addressee who might appear to be a female figure may not be necessarily so but also a figure of the divine kind. The neutrality of gender and the interchangeability of the male, female, and the divine is what makes the ghazal a complex site for the negotiation of meaning. While translating the ghazals, I have tried to identify this figure as a female in a traditional manner but it could be equally possible to identify the same one as a male figure, or a divine being. This mutability underlines the unique tradition of ghazal which projects the profane and the pious, the secular and the sacred, the plebeian and the patrician in a complex web of human associations with diverse manifestations of life and the possible meanings associated with them.

Putting together this volume has been a prolonged affair of love undertaken with some pain, some perseverance, and some patience but always with pleasure.

Anisur Rahman

SHUKRIYA

The idea of putting together the best of Urdu ghazals from the very beginnings to the present times in a single comprehensive volume of its own kind was appreciated and endorsed by many poets, possible readers and translators. They joined hands with me and helped me to put together this volume.

Thanks are due in particular to:

Rekhta Foundation website www.rekhta.org for the material accessed, as required.

Shamim Hanfi, Farhat Ehsas, Safdar Imam Quadri and Kauser Mazhari for helping me with the selection of poets and their ghazals.

Keki N. Daruwalla, Tabish Khair, Debjani Chatterjee, Janet Wilson, K. Satchidanandan, H. Masud Taj and Smita Agarwal for reading the translations and offering their suggestions.

Shantanu Ray Chaudhuri for his support.

Sohini Basak, my editor at HarperColllins and a poet in her own right, for making the book as it is.

Tabassum, Yasser, Munazzah, Tabrez, Maria, Mati and Obaid for sustaining me all through, as always, and Rabee for keeping me spirited in many ways.

*

The translator and publisher gratefully acknowledge the kind permission granted by the poets, or their publishers, to include their ghazals in this anthology. All efforts have been made to contact and seek permission from them to include their work in this collection. The publishers will, however, be pleased to make amends in case of inadvertent omissions, as the case may be.